MW01258688

I

*The Artisan Teaching Model*
*for Instructional Leadership*

"Baum and Krulwich's **Artisan Teaching** is a great example of the power of collaboration in schools. The **Artisan Teaching** model makes people better and should be widely emulated by those interested in building capacity and improving schools. Great ideas for creating a school community based in deep learning that benefits all schools."

**Michael Fullan**
Professor Emeritus, University of Toronto
Author of *Leading in a Culture of Change* and *Change Leader*

"**Artisan Teaching** *puts the emphasis right where it belongs—on the home-grown, teacher-led creation and improvement of* course curriculum and instruction. Baum and Krulwich's book, based on the excellent results achieved at their school in the Bronx, confirms the unrivaled power of focusing on the right things, all the time."

**Mike Schmoker**
Author of *Focus* and *Leading with Focus*

"At the Urban Assembly School for Applied Math and Science, Baum and Krulwich were leaders of one of the most successful new schools in New York City. Baum and Krulwich's system is a powerful and innovative new approach to leadership development within schools. Their model is both bold and creative and can be implemented successfully in any school in the country. It is a must-read for anyone interested in school improvement and in creating high-quality school leaders."

**Joel Klein**
Former Chancellor,
New York City Department of Education

"There are multiple pathways to creating fine public schools in highly challenged neighborhoods. Do read about this one, because this school truly honors teaching and teachers. Teamwork and embedded leadership nurture fine pedagogy: the result is at once humane and results in highly effective learning for students."

**Dr. David M. Steiner**
Executive Director, Johns Hopkins Institute for Education Policy
Former Commissioner, New York State Education Department

"We urgently need more schools like the one described in **Artisan Teaching**. In this important book, Baum and Krulwich show how to take teachers from apprentice to master—much like the most successful professional learning that occurs in other fields such as medicine, law, engineering, and architecture. Their structures and systems create critical opportunity for teachers to work deeply on their craft, recognizing that adult learning is absolutely essential for student learning. It's time that we stop looking for short cuts, add-ons, and quick fixes. **Artisan Teaching** is a bold, effective approach that elevates the teaching profession and moves us forward toward lasting improvement."

**Dr. Jal Mehta**
Associate Professor,
Harvard University Graduate School of Education

"Baum and Krulwich's model not only focuses teachers on student learning but also gets teachers truly excited about their own education. I highly recommend this book to those interested in building excellence in schools."

**Deborah Meier**
Senior Scholar,
New York University's Steinhardt School of Education
Author of *The Power of Their Ideas:
Lessons to America from a Small School in Harlem* and *In Schools We Trust*

# THE ARTISAN
# TEACHING
# MODEL FOR INSTRUCTIONAL LEADERSHIP

# THE ARTISAN
# TEACHING
# MODEL FOR INSTRUCTIONAL LEADERSHIP

*Working Together to Transform Your School*

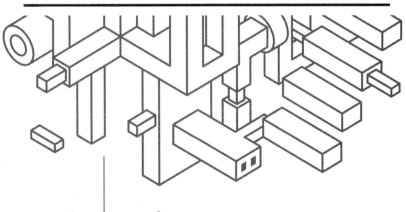

Kenneth
**BAUM**

David
**KRULWICH**

**ASCD**  Alexandria, VA USA

1703 N. Beauregard St. • Alexandria, VA 22311-1714 USA
Phone: 800-933-2723 or 703-578-9600 • Fax: 703-575-5400
Website: www.ascd.org • E-mail: member@ascd.org
Author guidelines: www.ascd.org/write

Deborah S. Delisle, *Executive Director*; Robert D. Clouse, *Managing Director, Digital Content & Publications*; Stefani Roth, *Publisher*; Genny Ostertag, *Director, Content Acquisitions*; Julie Houtz, *Director, Book Editing & Production*; Jamie Greene, *Editor*; Lindsey Smith, *Graphic Designer*; Mike Kalyan, *Manager, Production Services*; Andrea Wilson, *Senior Production Specialist*; Valerie Younkin, *Production Designer*

PAPERBACK ISBN: 978-1-4166-2251-2     ASCD product #116041     n8/16

PDF E-BOOK ISBN: 978-1-4166-2253-6; see Books in Print for other formats.

Quantity discounts: 10–49, 10%; 50+, 15%; 1,000+, special discounts (e-mail programteam@ascd.org or call 800-933-2723, ext. 5773, or 703-575-5773). For desk copies, go to www.ascd.org/deskcopy.

**Library of Congress Cataloging-in-Publication Data**
Names: Baum, Kenneth, author. | Krulwich, David.
Title: The artisan teaching model for instructional leadership : working together to transform your school / Kenneth Baum and David Krulwich.
Description: Alexandria, Virginia : ASCD, [2016] | Includes bibliographical references and index.
Identifiers: LCCN 2016018792 (print) | LCCN 2016030716 (ebook) | ISBN 9781416622512 (pbk.) | ISBN 9781416622536 (PDF e-book) | ISBN 9781416622536 (PDF)
Subjects: LCSH: Motivation in education. | Effective teaching. | Educational Leadership. | School improvement programs.
Classification: LCC LB1065 .B384 2016 (print) | LCC LB1065 (ebook) | DDC 371.102—dc23
LC record available at https://lccn.loc.gov/2016018792

23  22  21  20  19  18  17  16                    1  2  3  4  5  6  7  8  9  10  11  12

# THE ARTISAN TEACHING MODEL FOR INSTRUCTIONAL LEADERSHIP

*Working Together to Transform Your School*

# Introduction:
# A School Built with a New Vision

The model of teacher and leader development presented in this book originated at the Urban Assembly School for Applied Math and Science (AMS), a high-achieving public secondary school located in the middle of the poorest congressional district in the United States. Founded in 2004 during the small-school initiative in New York City, the school has no celebrity backers, no special dispensations, and no admission hurdles—it is a school truly open to all. And it has for over a decade offered a superb college-preparatory experience for students in grades 6 through 12 in the South Bronx. The school has received national and local recognition for high results, enriched instruction, and innovative school organization. In any given year, the school sends 85 percent of its graduates to two- and four-year colleges, almost all of them the first member of their families to attend college. That's impact, not just on students and families but on the whole community.

As the first and second principals of AMS, we are naturally proud of this record and of the difference the school has made in the lives of its students, its teachers, and the wider community. But in our view, what makes the school unique is its almost singular dedication to a vision of *teaching as a craft*. During an era of high-stakes testing and regimented behavior—for both students *and* teachers—AMS has focused on neither. We believe that standardized tests and associated metrics can be helpful, yet we put little effort toward test prep. We believe that student data can inform instruction, but we do not have extensive conversations around standards and data. We believe that calling students "scholars" won't make them any more scholarly, hanging collegiate banners won't make them any more college focused, and sending them to the dean won't improve their classroom behavior. We do not implement schoolwide discipline systems that force silence, and we do not support scripted lesson plans that take the curricular work out of the hands of newer teachers. Both of these not-uncommon practices, in our view, actually *hinder* the development of great teachers and instructional leaders, and they mask issues necessary for adult learning.

Above all, we believe in the power of an *artisan teacher*—one who consistently engages students in lessons that are simultaneously compelling, rigorous, supportive, and fun. The innovative structures at AMS—many of which run counter to current trends—were designed to virtually guarantee that every single teacher will improve every single day. To prize, above all, the well-taught class allows school leaders to give both teachers and students what they deserve. We want our students rushing to school because their math projects are interesting to them—not because they fear punishment and not because their presence will get them a pizza party. Students rushing to class because they want to learn—*this* is the hallmark of an artisan teacher. Although artisan teachers in our experience almost always get excellent standardized test scores relative to their peers and with similar students, test results are not a primary or real-time indicator of artisanship. The real primary indicators can be found in the classroom conversations: how students lean in with their own probing questions, debate or interpret texts, and apply mathematics to understand the world around them.

Similarly, we want our teachers excited about school not just because they enjoy helping children learn and because they know that high-quality teaching creates opportunity (both important) but also because the school experience is powerful for themselves as learners. Significant adult learning that occurs daily—as it does in the process of creating artisan teachers—is the impetus behind our school design. Traditionally, schools create a set of systems, with each one responsible for a desired outcome—such as the discipline system that generates desirable behavior or data analysis meetings that inform instruction. Schools then try to blend or otherwise coordinate these systems. At AMS, we wanted every desirable outcome—academic or behavioral—to be derived directly from well-taught classes. Achieving this singleness of purpose would require significant qualitative and quantitative changes to any of the school organization models known to us. Hence, we created our own.

At AMS, we have broken down and rebuilt all of these distinct structures into a single vehicle that provides the same supports authentically and collaboratively through the planning, revision, and analysis of daily lessons. This new structure respects and honors the *craft of teaching* and allows a school to focus on what matters most—students joyfully and authentically navigating rich, challenging, and worthwhile tasks. It requires a patient, long-term vision and an acute attention to and investment in adult development, such as we provide for the newer members of all other professions. It requires a school to engage all teachers every day with a team of artisans (and future artisans) who collaboratively take ownership of the success of the students they teach.

## Origins of the Model

When Kenneth Baum founded AMS in 2004 in a temporary space in the basement of a Bronx apartment building, he bought no textbooks and delivered no curriculum to the new teachers. Instead, he opened the school with a focus on the premise that later evolved into the Artisan Teaching model—that every teacher should collaboratively plan and debrief every day's lesson with at least one other teacher; that every one of the collaborative planning or debriefing sessions must be supported by a leader with a rich and inspirational view of great teaching; and that lessons should be compelling, rigorous, supportive, and fun.

In the early years, the school was so small that it could not provide many of the supports that teachers at larger schools take for granted. There were no deans, no assistant principals, and no professional development workshops. In a practical sense, the teachers at the brand-new

AMS only had time for this one job; both by design and by necessity, the small cadre of teachers spent their time collaboratively planning their curriculum. These "team meetings" where they planned these lessons quickly became the lifeblood of the school—they became the mentoring process, professional development, feedback sessions, and data meetings. These early team meetings became an all-encompassing apprenticeship for the new AMS teachers who were building the new school.

As the school grew, the Artisan Teaching model expanded and grew more refined. AMS quickly grew to serve over 600 students in grades 6 through 12 with a staff of 50 teachers. In the ensuing decade, AMS has earned sustained high ratings on all local measures, received a national award from Intel for school innovation, and achieved the highest rating possible for all of its New York City school-quality reviews. The school serves a heterogeneous population—20 percent with special needs, 10 percent English language learners, and over 90 percent receiving a free or reduced-price lunch—and it has demonstrated success for both its lower-achieving students (with a four-year graduation rate over 90 percent) and its high-achieving students (with one of the highest rates of college readiness and college matriculation of any non-screened school in New York City). Since its inception, the school has hired all of its instructional leaders from within, and the school has consistently generated more new leaders than available positions to fill.

Over the years, the school added an arts program with courses in visual art, music, dance, and drama; theme-based electives in architecture, engineering, and astronomy; and a wide-ranging hiking and camping program across all grade levels. Now located in a new building, AMS has developed seven years of curriculum, serving general education students, students with special needs, and English language learners. Five classes of students have graduated from 12th grade and moved on to postsecondary schools and careers. AMS teacher teams have built a schoolwide advisory program serving the social-emotional needs of students across all grade levels. The school runs a program of home visits in which the teachers new to AMS visit the homes of all incoming students during August in order to introduce themselves and welcome the families into the AMS community. The school has added after-school programs and sports teams, intensive support programs for struggling and at-risk students, and a middle school summer day camp open to all of its students.

While the school continues to evolve in so many important ways, the primary focus of school leaders throughout has been to expand, adjust, and develop the Artisan Teaching system. The collaborative planning teams and the development of instructional Team Leaders remain at the heart of the school—and the leaders have never wavered from the belief that the success of the school depends almost entirely on the success of this new model for supporting teachers. The Artisan Teaching model is rooted in over a decade of experience: it is a school structure that is tested and successful—and we believe it is also replicable and scalable.

## A Note About Supportive Research

Our work in formulating and implementing an innovative structure at a neighborhood school in the South Bronx was not rooted in an exhaustive analysis of the research on school design and teacher development. As school leaders, we devised, and then revised and adjusted, our ideas over the course of 12 years of on-the-job experience at AMS.

Nevertheless, the Artisan Teaching model does find support in educational research—albeit indirectly—in several interrelated ideas and philosophies. A comprehensive research study published by The New Teacher Project (TNTP) in 2015 concludes that bold solutions are needed:

> We believe districts should take a radical step toward upending their approach to helping teachers improve—from redefining what "helping teachers" really means to taking stock of current development efforts to rethinking broader systems for ensuring great teaching for all students.... Much of this work involves creating the conditions that foster growth, not finding quick-fix professional development solutions. (p. 3)

A large body of research has highlighted the value of professional collaboration among teachers. Many important writings have discussed "professional learning communities" (PLCs) and their importance in schoolwide structures for professional support. This philosophy focusing on collaboration is described in works such as Richard DuFour and Michael Fullan's *Cultures Built to Last* (2013) and Robert Marzano and Richard DuFour's *Leaders of Learning* (2011). The Artisan Teaching model rests in part on a similar view of the need for adult collaboration, but it expands the notion into a singular school structure built around sharing the work of teachers on small grade- and subject-specific teams.

Similarly, substantial research describes new models for sustainable school leadership. Several recent works have highlighted distributed leadership and the development of teacher leadership within schools—for example, Robert Marzano's *School Leadership That Works* (2005), James Spillane's *Diagnosis and Design for School Improvement: Using a Distributed Perspective to Lead and Manage Change* (2011), and Douglas Reeves's *The Learning Leader* (2006).

Marzano analyzes 21 leadership practices to consider those that affect student achievement the most; Spillane suggests that leaders focus on diagnosing the specific needs of their schools as they implement reforms; and Reeves suggests a leadership paradigm that focuses on the study of the "antecedents" for organizational success. We suggest a different shift in the daily tasks of instructional leaders—that they spend their time jointly engaged with teachers (and other leaders) in the daily work, collaborating intensely every day with a small number of teachers. We suggest a paradigm shift in which each leader simultaneously collaborates with and guides a small number of teachers in learning to teach one subject at one grade level superbly rather than the traditional model that focuses leaders' time on providing training sessions and feedback to all teachers in the school. AMS has no schoolwide (or even gradewide) focus for professional development and no time when all teachers are working on the same general goals such as "increasing accountable talk" or "improving questioning."

While consistent with research-based notions of collaborative team structures and distributed leadership, the Artisan Teaching approach is new. As noted by TNTP, the most common systems for training and improving the work of teachers *are not working*. In an article in the *Harvard Business Review*, Laurie Bassi and Daniel McMurrer (2007) analyzed the impact of various leadership techniques on student achievement in Beaufort County, South Carolina. The authors conclude that school leaders should not focus their efforts on exhaustive analysis of learning standards and data. Rather, their research indicates that student achievement improves most when leaders focus on the systematic engagement of adults in improving their practice. In a powerful conclusion similar to that of the TNTP report, Bassi and McMurrer state the following:

> Our results revealed that the school district's traditional emphasis on teaching to state standards had less to do with student performance than did the teachers' overall work and learning culture, the schools' ability to reinforce and retain talent.... This finding challenged most people's assumptions about the role of [school and district] leadership in creating successful work and learning environments. (Bassi & McMurrer, 2007, para. 25)

A look across this research suggests that school leaders need new structures that reorganize the work of teachers and leaders around authentic, day-to-day collaboration in teams—similar to the work of professionals in many other fields. Lee Shulman, former president of the Carnegie Center for the Advancement of Teaching and Learning, was one of the early proponents of bringing to teacher training the salient features of the medical training model. In 2005, Shulman concluded

> In [all] medical schools, in really good engineering programs, in seminaries, [students of the profession] have to act [with the experts as part of a team] ... and apply it in practice. In clinical medicine, the clinical team deliberates and agrees on an intervention with the patient, the action is taken, and the team returns the next day and to monitor progress and change. The medical

student or intern or resident stays with the patient during the intervening time, and comes back and reports. (p. 19)

Shulman called for teacher training to reflect "a larger, generic pedagogy of design, experiment, evaluate, and redesign engaged collectively and collaboratively [with experts] with lots of visibility, engagement, passion, and accountability among all members of the learning group." He calls this the language of "signature pedagogies."

Although many educators have embraced the notion of team-based collaboration (witness the proliferation of the PLC), these teams often engage in activities that are distinctly disconnected from the important daily work of planning and delivering instruction. Team members do not regularly design or redesign collectively and collaboratively with experts. They do not engage in the signature pedagogy. Instead, they look at data, unpack standards, and comb through quizzes, tests, and papers looking for nuances or trends. To be sure, looking at data and student work can be helpful, but without the presence of signature pedagogy as observed in other fields, teachers will not improve at the rate or in the way we need.

Similarly, recent analysis by Mike Schmoker urges school leaders to focus their time on what matters most: well-crafted curriculum and high-quality reading and writing instruction. Schmoker contends that these priorities are far more important—and yield stronger achievement results—than other practices currently in vogue (Schmoker, 1999, 2011). At AMS, we merged the idea of *teamwork* with the separate concept of the *artisan-apprentice relationship*. In an apprenticeship, newer members of a profession work alongside experts (the "artisans"), sometimes for many years, while the work is done. Over time, the apprentices gradually take on larger and more substantial roles—but always engaging in the work alongside, and *together with*, the artisans—as they become more skilled. This fusion of the concepts of teamwork and apprenticeship into a single vehicle for instructional leadership became the Artisan Teaching model. Our aim in the chapters that follow is to inspire you to learn and then implement this model into your own school.

# 1

## The Foundation

Artisan Teaching is based on this seemingly simple principle: great teachers make the difference. Great teachers are those who engage all students in compelling, rigorous activities that require higher-order thinking and allow them to articulate understandings verbally and in writing. They inspire children to do new and difficult work, make learning relevant to students' lives, and still leave time for practice. They get students to think critically while inspiring confidence and building intellectual habits, as well as constructing, debating, and solving problems. Great teachers inspire on a daily basis, allowing students to have confidence in their own abilities, and measurable achievement results typically follow.

It's a truism supported by the latest research that students—not just the administrators who observe—know who the great teachers are (Gates Foundation, 2013). The students of great teachers cannot wait for the lesson to begin because they know that they will learn and have fun doing so. They behave appropriately because they choose to and because they are too busy to be sidetracked by distractions. The students of great teachers are engaged, they are energetic and working as hard as they can, and they take risks and willingly try new things. Great teachers accomplish these things wherever they teach—in any neighborhood, with any population of students, and regardless of students' achievement level when they arrive. Great teachers see success in students with disabilities and those without, with students who speak English at home and those who do not. Great teachers know that, regardless of a student's knowledge and abilities in September, every student can make progress by June. Finally, great teachers also provide social and emotional support for their students—they get to know their students personally and support them when they need help with issues that are not directly related to the classroom.

This concept of teaching—that it is among the most challenging and also the most rewarding of professions—is complex and nuanced. To become a great teacher is an aspirational goal that is difficult to achieve. School leaders must begin with this foundation, and they must consider the types of school structures and systems that will help teachers move toward this vision. As Malcolm Gladwell (2011) points out, greatness in any skill or profession requires at least 10,000 hours of deep dedication and practice—and teaching is no different.

Although rubrics and checklists of actions may serve as "hallmarks" of good teaching, these actions, without more, do not make a great teacher. Teaching, indeed, is a craft. Great teachers must be treated as the artisans that they are, and school leaders must carefully consider the structures and supports necessary to develop artisanship within their schools.

The first step for a school leader executing the Artisan Teaching model is to articulate a strong, clear, and consistent instructional vision that values the importance, difficulty, and artistry of the work. The role of the leader is to hold on to this vision tenaciously and to gradually and methodically spread that instructional vision throughout the school. The leader cannot be distracted by short-term pressures and demands and cannot allow other priorities to overshadow the development of great teaching in the school. This belief in the importance of great teaching must precede any discussion of numerical outcomes, the percentage of students meeting standards, or the pace of reading-level changes. These metrics are part of—but not foundational to—a school that develops great teachers.

## The Three Pillars: Expertise, Collaboration, and Time

With the underlying premise that teaching is a craft and that schools must develop true artisanship, what is required to allow this work to succeed?

What are the conditions that allow greatness to happen? How do we foster the development of artisan teachers? The role of school leaders is to create the three conditions—the pillars—that allow this craftsmanship to develop: (1) expertise, (2) collaboration, and (3) time.

## Pillar 1: Expertise

The foundation of expertise is the ability to define and then consistently articulate a vision of great instruction—this is what will ultimately define the school. To achieve this pillar, a school must have at least one instructional leader who is an *expert* in all four of the following areas:

- academic content
- pedagogy
- youth development
- adult learning and locus of control

It is not good enough to have this expertise distributed among the members of a leadership team. Lee Shulman (2005), in his synthesis of what he called pedagogical content knowledge, has argued that content and pedagogy are deeply intertwined and that to treat the two as essentially mutually exclusive misses critical interplay between the two. We agree. Furthermore, when we get into teacher development, we believe that adult learning is in part a function of mindset. For example, a teacher's reluctance to try to engender higher-order thinking may stem from not knowing how (a combination of pedagogy and content), or it may stem from a (mistaken) belief that students do not have the ability, that it is beyond the teacher's "locus of control." Teasing this out can at times be difficult. A parallel situation can exist with youth development. A teacher (or administrator) may believe that students "can't handle" project-based or inquiry lessons, when the real issue is that the teacher has yet to become proficient at fostering student relationships and misses key aspects of youth development. Although learning specialists and content specialists can bring value, content mastery and teaching techniques often fall flat without a positive learning environment established, we believe, through respectful and authentic relationships—not with regimented behavior. Again, the issue may not be a lack of knowledge (pedagogy or content) or even a lack of willingness (locus of control) but a lack of understanding of youth development. Good teacher-student relationships—where students increasingly and consistently make wise choices—are critical to Artisan Teaching.

At any one time, in any classroom, it is almost always the case that there is no one issue, and often it is the complex relationship among these issues that makes deep teacher improvement both so hard and so satisfying. It is seldom about the "right teacher move" by itself, the lack of teacher content knowledge, and the like. It is the inherent interrelatedness of these issues that makes the work of significantly improving teaching so difficult. Therefore, it won't work to sequentially call in the content specialist to fill gaps in content, then call in the behavior specialist to fix student behavior, then call in the supervisor to fix the adult mindset, and so forth. This sequential approach often displaces issues rather than solving them.

For these reasons, we believe that any leader responsible for improvement of teachers must be expert in all four areas. Such leaders are called Team Leaders at AMS, and each of these Team Leaders designs, organizes, and influences almost all of the adult learning for a small group of teachers through the all-important team meetings (fully described later in the book). Defining the Team Leader role in this way has implications, examined further in Chapter 3, for other key school roles and assignments. For example, the "dean of discipline" does not attend these meetings or handle the so-called difficult kid issues for each team. The Team Leader does. There is no separate history expert who owns and clarifies key historical concepts and who then dispenses closely held knowledge. The Team Leader does. And generally, there is no supervisor who handles teachers that externalize and don't take responsibility for improvement. The Team Leader does.

## Pillar 2: Collaboration

Next, certain structures and systems need to be put in place to enable experts to collaborate effectively with other teachers in the school.

Craftsmanship is developed when newer or less-proficient members of the profession work together on the job with the experts. The standard preservice experience of student teaching can be helpful in a limited way, but student teaching does not accomplish the growth of artisans for several reasons. First, these experiences generally have a short duration, making any significant adult growth unlikely. Second, the supervising teacher, who is responsible and accountable for student growth in that classroom, is likely to deal with tensions that need to be experienced and learned by the new practitioner. Rarely would a supervising teacher let the classroom react authentically to the new teacher for any significant period because it might have consequences for the supervising teacher and students. As such, the student teacher often gets a false sense of the true classroom dynamic he or she will feel when taking the helm for the first time. Moreover, the student teacher is too safe: he or she is neither accountable nor responsible for the results of the teaching experience. As such, the experience is inauthentic—there is no real risk from the student teacher's perspective because his or her work is not the work that really matters. It is this risk, tied to the success or failure of an important outcome, that is necessary for meaningful adult growth.

Thus, on-the-job expert-novice collaboration is needed, but how can you get this collaboration in schools? The fiscal realities of locally funded districts in the United States almost always dictate one teacher per classroom. In Chapter 4, we show how we have generated a powerful collaboration—one that successfully creates artisans—through effective and highly intentional organization. In this organization, all nonteaching time gets repurposed, traditional professional development workshops are eliminated, job responsibilities of some classic leadership positions are changed dramatically, long-established efficiencies that characterize most modern school schedules are abandoned, and the critical Artisan Teaching team system is defined and described.

## Pillar 3: Time

Finally, the work of training artisans takes time. If we had only two or three years with teachers before they moved on to their "real" careers, we could not implement the Artisan Teaching model. With a short teaching horizon, investment in developing artisans won't pay off. Similarly, using short-term human resource strategies with teachers you expect to stay 7, 8, or 12 years also does not make sense. Our teachers stay because they feel like artisans who are constantly honing their craft. Their students don't always achieve great assessment results in their first or second year of teaching. But that is not our intent. Our intent is to create proud artisans who stay in the classroom and get students to become better critical and creative thinkers. Our aim is to graduate students who are well prepared intellectually and emotionally in the long term and who are prepared for college and career success. A byproduct is that our students score extremely well on all sorts of measures, including standardized tests.

As we explain in detail in Chapter 6, true success in these areas requires a deliberate and dramatic repurposing of a teacher's typical week. Central to our vision of developing artisans is the formation of microprofessional learning communities that continually work together to improve instruction. Every lesson plan is discussed, challenged, and improved, and then it is taught by more than one teacher. Every difficult issue that a teacher faces becomes part of a wider discussion among his or her teammates and mentors. Every new teacher shares the stress and difficulty of the new profession with at least one veteran who supports that teacher on a daily basis. In every discussion, both mentors and mentees are present and learning from each other—indeed, everyone is learning.

The confluence of expertise, collaboration, and time creates meaningful collaboration that is neither quick nor easy, requiring a major commitment on behalf of the entire organization. The collaborative relationship must serve as the central, defining feature of the school's system for hiring, training, mentoring, and professional development. In school systems where teachers and administrators are too often burdened by time constraints, a school must make fundamental, structural changes to the way it functions to create the time necessary to achieve this goal.

## The Organization of This Book

Part I opens with three chapters in which we discuss how AMS created its Artisan Teaching system to help develop teachers into great craftspeople. The goal was to train teachers in a collegial, supportive manner, working together in teams. In doing so, we sought to provide a system of support for newer members of the profession that parallels those in many other professions and that treats the "craft of teaching" with the respect that it deserves. This collaborative team system requires a rethinking of many of the supports that schools normally provide for teachers. It requires a restructuring of roles and the time teachers and administrators spend on various tasks.

In Chapter 2, we look more closely at the four areas of expertise that comprise the craft of teaching and at the development of the artisan teachers who serve as teacher leaders in the Artisan Teaching apprenticeship model.

In Chapter 3, we describe the processes that allow the Artisan Teaching model to function smoothly and how they are necessitated and supported by the underlying philosophy of the approach.

Chapter 4 looks at how the model plays out over time and results in student success. As teachers progress through this system, they learn how to work effectively with others on a team; they learn how to support other teachers with less experience; they learn how to mentor and share their expertise; they learn how to observe and provide feedback; they learn how to develop a strong internal locus of control; and they work with a variety of different teachers, all with different successes, struggles, and learning styles. They learn all of this over the course of several years of teaching, even before they begin any formal role in school leadership.

In Chapter 5, we discuss another important result of the focused, embedded professional development provided within the apprenticeship system: teachers are simultaneously learning to teach and learning to lead. In designing a system to improve classroom teaching by focusing on rich, authentic, and intensive collaboration among teachers, we also set in motion a system that trains teachers to step into new roles as the school's instructional leaders. The Artisan Teaching system accomplishes both objectives at the same time—and results in an overflowing pipeline of well-qualified leaders.

In the second part of the book, we present a blueprint and strategies on how to bring the Artisan Teaching model to any school—big, small, urban, rural, district, or charter. Each chapter closes with one or more frequently asked questions that we have received over the past several years.

In Chapter 6, we show how to free up the time to create the structures and systems for implementation. We provide suggested time reallocations for key personnel and suggested changes to traditional roles and responsibilities. We also offer solutions to programming challenges and include sample schedules to ground the work in the day-to-day operations and realities of running a school.

In Chapter 7, we display the flexibility of implementation by detailing several strategies that can be employed given a wide variety of school conditions. For example, we explain how implementation is actually easier in larger schools. Strategies are given to implement all at once or gradually over time by either grade or subject.

In Chapter 8, we address the most frequently asked question we have received to date: "Can all teachers benefit from this system?" or its companion question "Do certain teachers benefit more in this system, and how do you find teachers to fit the model?" Even though we are certain that this system can help all teachers and make many of them into artisans, we also firmly believe that certain character traits are ideal. Although these traits are not in and of themselves original to us, what we have done over the years is develop a hiring process—counterintuitive and unique—that does a reliable job of identifying these future artisans. In this chapter, we share what we have learned about hiring, detailing every step of what it takes to hire future artisans.

# Chapter 1

**Question:** *Your book begins with a description of your view of great teaching. Does the leadership model and structure that you describe require us to agree with your teaching philosophy? Will your model be effective if I believe in a different style of teaching or have a different belief about instruction?*

**Answer:** Yes and no. We are not suggesting that everyone must agree precisely with our view of great instruction. Schools have different themes and missions, and every school is at a different stage of its instructional development. We think it is important for school leaders to articulate their own view of great teaching, tailored to their own school's needs. We are not suggesting a need for uniformity across different schools and communities.

The important premise underlying the remainder of this book, however, is that the focus of instructional leaders must be rooted in the quality and richness of classroom instruction and not on something else. The mission driving the school leaders must be for great teaching to serve as the basis for all that follows. Data, student assessment results, college readiness, and good behavior must be viewed as the results of great instruction—not as the underlying mission in itself.

As long as you can articulate the school mission in a way that is focused on the nature of the classroom teaching—how it looks, sounds, and feels—the specific details of that vision can vary. But not every description passes scrutiny. If a school leader believes that great teaching is a classroom where "every child masters the daily standard by successfully answering an 'exit ticket' at the end of class," this is not a mission rooted in Artisan Teaching but rather a mission rooted in outcomes—and simple ones at that. If that is the extent of the school leader's mission for teachers, then there is no point in implementing the system set forth in this book. We hope our students will master the standards, too, but implementing the Artisan Teaching approach requires constant discussion and collaboration around the instruction, not the outcomes.

# PART I

## The Artisan Teaching Model

# 2

## The Elements of Expertise: Who Are the Leaders?

In the Artisan Teaching system, each team has a Team Leader (TL) who drives the collaborative relationship and, as such, needs to embody qualities that can accelerate the development of teaching as a craft. The TLs are grown from within the school. As teachers participate on the collaborative team, talented hard workers begin to emerge and find themselves on track to become TLs who, in exchange for a reduced teaching assignment, lead groups of teachers and become responsible for teacher and leader development.

How does a school create a TL from a teacher, either new or experienced? The first step is to be completely transparent with the entire school about the qualifications, explaining that the sustainability of the school depends on a certain number of teachers emerging into leadership. We have broken up the process to becoming a TL into three stages (explained in this chapter) that we describe to the entire faculty even before they embark on their career with us.

The approach is therefore transparent and provides precisely the same support for all teachers—even those who don't ultimately become Team Leaders still receive the same rich development and support. This is support that all teachers deserve. Though the program is egalitarian by structure, it is a meritocracy in leadership output. Years of service do not get you the job of TL—excellence does, and there is no hiding this intention from the faculty. Transparency is key, and when a new Team Leader is named, the sentiment among the faculty is almost universally one of "that makes perfect sense." This is not to say that some are not disappointed, but it's better to have people potentially fall short in clear pursuit of excellence than have people confused as to the goal. Those who don't make it initially to TL get rich, personalized development. They still might not get there, but the pursuit is well worth it to both the teacher and school.

Everyone, regardless of profession, needs to know at some level of detail what success looks like in their chosen careers. The earlier the better, we believe. From the moment they start work, we show teachers what this path looks like. Every teacher new to the school learns the three progressive stages of becoming a Team Leader.

---

**Stage 1: The Fundamentals of Teaching I.** You will take ownership of your room, take pride in keeping everyone inside your room, and learn the basics of classroom management. You will learn the curriculum thoroughly as the year progresses, and you will be reflective and thoughtful in your team meetings. You will demonstrate improved classroom management over the course of the year, develop a warm environment with clear routines, and receive strong formal observations that show steady improvement. You will demonstrate that you can consistently deliver a lesson in a teacher-directed, student-centered model that allows ample time for student practice. You consistently seek advice of excellent teachers. You participate in conversations about teaching and learning. You pop into the rooms of excellent teachers, show interest in pedagogy, and show a keen interest in student achievement. You aggressively work on the weakest part of your game rather than hiding from it. You will, undoubtedly, get frustrated with your students, but what you do with that frustration is key. You do not blame students. Rather, you understand completely that it is you. *You* are the work in progress; *you* are developing and transforming.

**Stage 2: The Fundamentals of Teaching II.** You refine your fundamentals, expand your teaching repertoire, and become much more aware of what students are thinking and learning. You continue toward excellence in classroom management. You deepen your knowledge of curriculum and pedagogy significantly. You expand your instructional repertoire to include methods of delivery such as Socratic seminars, debates, in-class games, and alternative assessments. Your test scores relative to first year are stronger. Your formal observations show that you have made progress and new goals have been identified. You bring a new depth to team meetings, showing significant thought on how to get students sharper. You add more to your team meetings than scope and sequence. You talk often about student achievement and how to push students to think more critically. You offer insights that move the instructional conversation in line with our school mission. Your students are almost always on task, you have developed excellent rapport with your students, and you are clearly pushing students to think critically with excellent questioning. You seek out troubled kids in the hallway just because you want to, even though you have enough to do already.

**Stage 3: The Acceleration.** It is absolutely clear and consistent by all metrics (e.g., formal observations, informal observations, student feedback, peer feedback, test scores, student work) that your students are improving at a high rate relative to your peer group. You regularly start conversations about teaching and learning, and you are focused on student achievement. You are self-critical and realize that now, with student behavior and the basics of teaching under control, you continue to push yourself to drive student achievement. You know that years 3 and 4 are about you pushing yourself. In doing so,

- You consistently get your class to produce solid work, tirelessly push all students in your room to achieve, and write terrific lesson plans. *But you are not satisfied.*
- Students say that you are tough, but they also say that they like your class. You consistently handle students that are considered difficult and get many of them to achieve. *But you are not satisfied.*

- You volunteer for at least two big projects around student achievement that require significant communication, leadership of teachers, and thought. You execute these projects well. Projects could be designing an entirely new course, running a portion of summer school, running a portion of Saturday school, programming the school, implementing an intervention group for 10 of the lowest achievers in a grade, and so forth. *But you are not satisfied.*
- Without asking, you help struggling/emerging teachers with nontrivial assistance (e.g., model a lesson after school). You understand entirely, and often articulate to the larger school community, the school's mission. You find yourself, three or four years into the job, with a strong desire to help other teachers. *But you are still not satisfied.*
- You want to be a team leader because you want more time to help other teachers get better.

**Minimum Team Leader Qualifications:** Minimum four years of full-time teaching experience. Possess superb instructional technique as evidenced by excellent formal teacher observations, test scores, and year-end ratings. Team Leaders will have made consistent and significant positive contributions to their academic teams. Team Leaders possess expertise in (1) academic content, (2) pedagogical techniques (instruction and assessment), (3) youth development (including student behavior and discipline), and (4) adult development and internal locus of control. In particular, they will have been largely responsible for the significant growth of a colleague in at least two of the four above areas. Ability to lead summer planning sessions prior to the start of the school year. Team Leaders are also problem solvers, consensus builders, and persons with demonstrated organizational ability and with a demonstrated history of meeting deadlines. Team Leaders move instructional conversations along, find common ground, and push everyone around them toward instructional excellence.

What enables a TL to develop teachers along this trajectory? Let's consider more carefully the four areas of expertise we require from Team Leaders: (1) academic content, (2) pedagogical techniques (instruction and assessment), (3) youth development (including student behavior and discipline), and (4) adult development and locus of control.

It is well established that an instructional leader must be an expert in academic content. For example, a TL who is developing a math teacher needs to know math well—but this is only the start. A TL in a school with rich instructional vision—especially in the era of the Common Core State Standards—needs to be able to make math connections easily and expertly to a multitude of areas of social, physical, and life sciences, as well as to the world of a teenager. He or she needs to be able to answer students' age-old question, "What is this stuff good for?" The TL needs to make sure that developing math teachers can and will answer this question for students *daily*.

---

**DIARY OF A TEACHER**
**Content Vignette 1**

*"Why would a 7th grader care about this?" said my Team Leader, Ms. Rodriguez. My teammate, Mr. Johnson, who also teaches two sections of 7th grade math, Ms. Rodriguez, and I were discussing a lesson that I wrote for an upcoming unit. I didn't know what to say. Ms. Rodriguez then encouraged me to talk through the lesson, explaining "where and why a 7th grader would really get excited." I explained that kids would solve for different side lengths, require multistep solutions, and include decimals and fractions. Ms. Rodriguez liked these points but said that she doubted whether a 12-year-old would do any of the problems I gave them unless they were told they had to. "You mean," I said, "that I need to come up with lessons that a kid would do even if no one told them they had to?" Rodriguez smiled. "That's the bar," she said, "day in and day out."*

A Team Leader in math does not need to have an advanced degree in mathematics or engineering but needs to be the kind of person who, walking past a newsstand, might pick up a copy of *Scientific American* just to read out of curiosity. He or she is the kind of person who, sitting at a Yankees game, can see the math all around—from the velocity of a fastball to the quadratic arc of a line drive, from the ratios of batting averages to the angles of the infield diamond, and from the Pythagorean (and irrational) distance from home plate to second base to the probability of a randomly chosen person in the upper deck catching a foul ball. One can have degrees in math or education and not see applications that are of interest to students. But to the Team Leader, these real-world connections are ubiquitous. This skill (which most definitely can be taught) is included in our definition of *content expertise*.

---

**DIARY OF A TEACHER**
**Content Vignette 2**

*"That's thinking like a kid!"* shouted my Team Leader, Ms. Rodri-guez, who was clearly excited. I had done my homework from the meeting yesterday—try to think like a 12-year-old and figure out what would excite him about the Pythagorean theorem. Rodriguez had encouraged me to think about the action-oriented world of a 7th grader and to come up with scenarios that are truly interesting to that student. It took me a while, but I came up with building a huge slip-and-slide from a second-floor window to a backyard lot, building a skateboard ramp, and making a zip line in a nearby park.

*As I was describing the Pythagorean zip line, we all started to get excited. I ran to the board, scribbled furiously, and showed how kids would need to measure the distance from the lake to the base of the tree and then connect the zip line from the lake to a branch in the tree. Johnson jumped in: "The kids could use a surveyor's* wheel to measure distance from lake to the base of tree—that's circumference! We could review that the day before!" Rodriguez added, "Yup, I see the triangle, but how would kids figure out the altitude of the tree limb?" Me: "I bet some kid would figure out that they could attach a rope to something heavy, throw it over the tree limb, and mark off the distance. Oh—that could be the Do-Now!" Johnson and I high-fived.

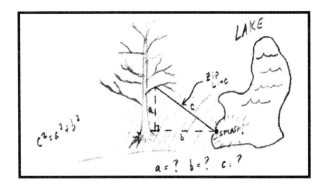

Rodriguez then asked me to weave in my "pure math" questions from the lesson I shared yesterday. I started writing questions: "What if the tree limb was 30 feet high as opposed to 25 feet high? Now what length cable do we need to get at Home Depot?" And "Suppose Home Depot only sells 200-foot cable. What altitude tree limb would we need to find?" and so on. Johnson: "Hold it—we've got a big problem here—no way are we allowed to zip-line a kid into the lake. Kids can't do this." Me: "No, but we can zip-line a stuffed animal into the lake, maybe one wearing the school uniform. Kids would be into that." Another high-five.

A Team Leader must be expert in pedagogy as well. TLs need to model creative, exciting instructional methods that bust out of the all-too-common, skills-based approach to teaching. These include Socratic seminars, classroom debates, purposeful theater, and other lesson deliveries that capitalize on imagination, link to other content areas, foster creativity, and inspire students to manipulate, conjecture, experiment, read rigorous texts, and write and revise with authentic purpose. The Team Leader needs to lead his or her team to deliver pedagogical techniques that inspire students to speak, read, and write effectively.

---

### DIARY OF A TEACHER
### Pedagogy Vignette

*"Go get 20 textbooks from the storeroom and meet me in the atrium in five minutes," Rodriguez said. This was how our after-school meeting started today. I used to think of lesson planning as teachers huddled at a desk in the staff room, reviewing standards and skills, combing through written resources, and looking stuff up on websites. We do some of that, but here I was, standing in the atrium of the school, prying up 100 pounds of stacked books. Rodriguez continued, "Now grab the lever twice as long, keep the same fulcrum location, and do the same thing. What are the key, deep questions to ask a student who is doing what you are doing right now? And what data does a kid need to collect to answer these questions?" This was a long way from the staff room. As I scanned the atrium, I saw my team assembling inclined planes, different class levers, pulleys—a veritable amusement park of mechanical advantage. Finally, Rodriguez asked me a question I didn't see in the teacher's editions of my textbooks: "How can I get 24 kids through these stations in 90 minutes without complete chaos?"*

---

Experts in pedagogy know how to provide real and effective supports for English language learners (ELLs) and students with learning disabilities—the TL must be able to help teachers differentiate for these learners, not by lowering standards but by creating a scaffold of supports that allow these students to master the same standards as their nondisabled or non-ELL peers. The TL must be expert in pedagogical techniques that cut across all student classifications. He or she must be expert in checking for understanding and know well, for example, that the commonplace practice of asking students to show a thumbs-up if they understand and a thumbs-down if they don't is entirely unreliable—if only it were that easy! Same for "fists of five" and other techniques that produce instantly quantifiable data (and dupe the teacher into thinking he or she is "using data to inform instruction") but that actually do not detect *any* understanding. Yes or no answers—whether verbal or a physical gesture such as a thumbs-up—do not tell teachers what students understand, and the TL should banish such false checks from his or her repertoire. The TL will be expert in legitimate checks for understanding, such as asking the right open-ended questions to the right students at the right time with astounding purposefulness and efficacy. The TL will be able to model this for the teachers he or she leads. In assessment, the TL can design tests that diagnose at a surgical level. Assessment becomes an art in and of itself, ranging from factual recall to application. The TL knows how to assess students to get a great sense of how they are progressing in thinking, and the TL teaches teachers how to construct assessments that show teachers what they need to improve in themselves. This is all part of pedagogical expertise.

---

**DIARY OF A TEACHER**
**Content Vignette 3**

*"Sorry, but this is boring. Why would a 16-year-old care about Archduke Ferdinand?"*

*My Team Leader, Mr. Thomas, was dissecting the lesson I wrote, an 11th grade lesson that started with students taking notes about the causes of World War I. Not sure what to say in response, I* offered, "This is one of the most important state standards, and isn't it on the state test each year?" Mr. Thomas replied, "That wasn't my question." There was a long pause while I thought about why a 16-year-old would care about Archduke Ferdinand. I thought quietly for about two minutes.

Finally, I answered. "It's about alliances! Teenagers experience this in their social cliques and when they stand up for their friends. Teenagers strategically form and dissolve intense alliances naturally and with almost daily frequency." Mr. Thomas quickly offered, "So is standing up for your friend the right thing to do? Is it a good decision to stand up for friends?" I said, "Of course," paused, and then added, "Wait, obviously it didn't work very well in World War I." Thomas: "When does standing up for your friends work?" Me: "I don't know. When it's something worth fighting for? Maybe when we leave a 'way out' before unimportant conflicts escalate?"

Mr. Thomas began explaining the idea of an "essential question" for a unit of study. We talked for 30 minutes about the students in my class, crafted questions, offered predictions about how my students would answer, and thought about what my follow-up questions should be. And then I was asked to generate follow-up questions to the follow-up questions. We went through six levels of follow-up questions before Mr. Thomas said, "Now, how can you structure this in a way that students want to and will ask these questions of one another?" Then there was another lull in the conversation while I thought for a few minutes, before I continued.

"What if our kids started the unit by writing about situations in their own lives where they stood up for a friend in an alliance? After writing, they could briefly act the scenarios out in groups, each time going deep with the decision-making process. Then we can debate the value of alliances—do they help us protect weaker members of the alliance, or do they cause conflicts to escalate needlessly as more allies jump into the fight? By looking at the alliances that exist in their lives, we could introduce and drive home key terms, such as domino effect, deterrence, and appeasement, and kids could take notes and define those terms as they arise. I could push the kids to distinguish a needless escalation, such as World War I, from a cause that can be viewed as more worthy, such as preventing genocide in World War II. Then we bounce back to the archduke and maybe afterward use the same essential question to explore Neville Chamberlain or the conflict in Vietnam. With each new conflict, well-chosen scenarios that the students wrote and acted out could lead the way!"

For a moment, let's return to the thumbs-up check for understanding. How many kids—due to their normal developmental stage—would choose to display a "thumbs-down" and visibly indicate that they are among the ones publicly tallied as "confused"? Very few. Teenagers do not like their misunderstandings broadcast to a classroom of peers, especially if it means that they will appear slow to get it. For sure, this is a "check for understanding issue," but it is also a youth development issue—the third major component of expertise. Artisan teachers understand deeply the developmental periods of the kids they teach and are keenly aware of—and instinctively avoid—situations where peer pressure and youth insecurity will work against them. Artisan teachers constantly keep in mind the very real social and emotional forces of a room (e.g., what embarrasses kids, what is safe to ask) and then manage teenage insecurities adroitly.

Artisans have a keen awareness of youth dynamics and motivations, and they then find incredibly resourceful ways to exploit this awareness. You can occasionally find these teachers in the lunchroom chatting with students—not every day but often enough to get noticed and often enough to let them know that they care on a personal level. Tweens, especially, eat this up, and this may be one of the quickest ways to get a difficult 12-year-old on your side.

But this approach can also extend directly to academics. Great secondary school teachers strategically group students not only by academic level (e.g., reading level) but also according to a host of other social forces. They consider when to separate students who are dating and when to ensure that rivals join opposite sides of academic debates. All of this ultimately increases students' time on task and ability to concentrate. Artisans understand that many teenagers are wired to think about teenage survival, which includes the effects of puberty, showing off, and bullying. All of this is going through many teenage brains while one is trying to teach them the forces that led to the Civil War or how to use a Bunsen burner. This is not to say that an academic class should turn into an advisory or a health class, but not considering what is biologically and emotionally happening to a student can leave huge blocks to learning in place. Great teachers know about natural teenage thoughts, respect them for their power, and design lessons that—in a very real way—become the most interesting and important stimuli in that teenager's world...at least for that hour of class.

Youth development, unfortunately, does not get much attention in the standardized test era. It is crucial to the work, however, as it informs the notion of student discipline. We take the view that most nonviolent student misbehaviors are not *bad*; they are *natural*. Talking out of turn, throwing a paper ball at a friend, and even disrespecting a teacher are examples of how healthy students test boundaries when they are faced with a lesson that is boring, too difficult, or otherwise unnecessarily frustrating. Both seeking behavioral limits and wanting not to be bored are healthy, normal, and appropriate child pursuits. This is the youth development awareness that every teacher must have in the Artisan Teaching system: student behavior can be greatly influenced by teachers who are aware of youth development. Of course, these misbehaviors at times need consequences. But consequences need to be given with great thought—not robotically—and levied most effectively by the teacher in the room, not by someone else. This means no classroom removals to the dean's office (except for the rare instances of violence or sexual harassment).

It is crucial to determine whether the offending behaviors would or would not happen in the classroom of a skilled teacher. If the same disruptive student in one teacher's room does not misbehave with an artisan teacher, then the only real issue is the skill level of the struggling teacher. In this case, punishing the student due to a "schoolwide zero tolerance" policy makes no sense—there is nothing schoolwide about the issue. The issue is that the teacher does not yet have the skills necessary to get consistently good behavior from students who are actually quite able to provide it. The teacher may choose to give this misbehaving student a sensible consequence, which may turn out to be helpful to this teacher getting better at classroom management. But the school assigning the consequence will not work. The student clearly respects the school but not the teacher (yet).

If most off-task activity and misbehavior stem from a lack of teacher proficiency (mountains of data support the fact that excellent teachers have significantly fewer behavior problems), and if students quite naturally start to test boundaries as they mature, and if a teacher is not yet skilled in dealing with students who are testing boundaries, then it makes no sense to have someone whom the student already respects swoop in and punish the student. It makes every sense in the world to swoop in and help that teacher learn to handle students who don't take direction easily. Removing the misbehaving student from the class not only is unfair to that student but also robs the teacher of the opportunity and responsibility to learn how to creatively deal with difficult students.

Teachers need to develop an expertise in youth development that leads them to reject the idea of tallying and tracking misbehavior to ultimately unload the offending student onto someone with much more perceived authority. We have seen this tactic devolve into a game of sorts for kids, seeing who can rack up more demerit points. Merit and demerit systems depersonalize and are unhelpful not just because they don't work but also because they make it harder to develop relationships with students. Great teachers rarely send their students to the dean's office for punishment because doing so undermines their credibility. More often than not, the message sent to the student is "you are not wanted"—a message that a future Team Leader would definitely want to avoid.

A quick note on serious misbehavior: we believe that the overwhelming majority of off-task behavior can be prevented through artisan teaching. There are exceptions, of course. There are students with serious emotional difficulties and various syndromes (that also benefit greatly from artisan teaching) who need additional social and emotional supports, including expert professional counseling.

Students want to pay attention and behave well for teachers who teach well and who, for lack of a better term, "get" them. This is a very important part of the craft of teaching. Students are wonderfully alive with personality and choice. Our hope is to build artisan teachers who are so good that, given the choice between misbehaving and not, students will consistently make the appropriate choice.

---

### DIARY OF A TEACHER
### Team Apprenticeship Meeting (October)

*I am struggling with classroom management. Kids are starting to push back, and I want desperately to send them to the dean, but I am not allowed! My friends at other schools get to send kids out when they act up—it doesn't seem fair. At my team meeting today, I spoke about the kids acting out, but I was quickly redirected to describe what I was doing when things went off-track. Rodriguez and Johnson told me that most likely I had taught over my kids' heads, that kids couldn't follow me and then got bored and acted out. When I said something like "these kids can't behave well," it was as if we were in a car traveling along that screeched to a stop. Rodriguez and Johnson immediately took me on a tour of the 7th*

> *grade classes going on. I saw the kids who gave me the hardest time perfectly well behaved in English class, then in art class, then in advisory. I was forced to see that the issue was not the kids. The issue was me.*

Within a few months, typically, teachers who develop a strong internal locus of control will see significant progress in their classrooms. Consider the following vignette:

> **DIARY OF A TEACHER**
> **Team Apprenticeship Meeting (February)**
>
> *I'm kind of stunned: for the first time, it seems like all of my kids were well behaved today. They did their work, and they were mostly on point. Even John—who I was convinced had dedicated his pre-teen years to trying to make me cry—got into his work today. When I shared this, Johnson and Rodriguez encouraged me to be very specific, but they did not seem surprised at how things went. They also did not seem surprised that I couldn't pinpoint one thing that made the difference. "Most likely, there was no one thing," Rodriguez said. "You have been doing the right things for months now," she continued. "It was an accumulation of things, and it takes a while—especially appearing 'believable' to kids—but remember that you did not send kids out and did not have an authority figure come in. Remember this, especially on your tougher days."*

This vignette highlights a teacher's shift in what she can control (i.e., developing an *internal* locus of control), perhaps the most critical of the Team Leader's four required areas of expertise. In this vignette, by wanting to send students to the dean, the teacher is essentially giving up her control of the situation. Not only has she been unable to get students to behave, but the solution she wants is for the dean to provide the discipline for her. Externalizing the locus of control is anathema to the Team Leader. Psychologist Carol Dweck (2007), who has written extensively about this subject using the language of "growth and fixed mindsets," has shown how debilitating a fixed mindset can be to organizations. In pushing organizations toward excellence, the fixed mindset must be countered and shifted.

A further look at the vignette actually shows a regression in adult development prior to the Team Leader taking action and getting the locus to shift. After the external solution (i.e., sending the student to the dean) is shot down, the teacher then tries to argue that the kids themselves are the limiting factor and that no one could improve the situation. That is a strong manifestation of a fixed mindset, and what the Team Leader did in this vignette in response shows an intense attenuation to locus of control. The Team Leader immediately shut the meeting down and on the spot took the teacher on an impromptu walk around the building to confront facts that would shake free the fixed mindset.

The TL's responsibility to guard against the forming of an externalized locus of control cannot be overstated and stems from the nature of the job of teaching. Given the real and numerous obstacles facing teachers—students who are years behind, students with disrupted home lives, absenteeism—and the fact that every teacher's workday consists of a thousand opportunities for students to make poor choices, the lure of externalization is powerful. Only the most vigilant who are constantly keeping these forces of externalization at bay are likely to emerge with the most powerful internal locus of control, the best of growth mindsets. The TL has a very tough job in this regard. Often, the TL is the single person who must hold the line and help his or her teachers tenaciously cling to a growth mindset. This is why the TL must deeply understand adult development and locus of control.

Setting an internal locus of control is also a major reason that a school following the Artisan Teaching model requires all newly hired teachers, as their very first professional responsibility at the school, to go on a week's worth of home visits. In the hands of a skilled Team Leader, this experience can be accessed over and over again to combat the fixed mindset.

> **DIARY OF A TEACHER**
> **Team Apprenticeship Meeting (Home Visits in August)**
>
> *Sitting in the living room of a 6th grader's apartment in the Webster Avenue housing projects in the South Bronx, I listened intently to the family's immigrant story. This week, along with three other teachers new to the school, I visited incoming 6th grade students and families in their homes. We spoke to four families a day, five days in a row. I was given talking points but not a script. I had known for a while that I wanted to teach, but I had not yet been forced to think about how I fit into the big picture. As I scanned the room, I spotted articles of hope and pride—a Little League trophy, a framed "best attendance" award—and I wondered what I owed to a community where most kids never make it through high school. I started talking about support, and then I said to the mother, "I owe it to your son to become a terrific teacher—to have lessons that make your son want to come to school and that help him become a better thinker."*

**Chapter 2**

**Question:** *My school already has a system for identifying the best teachers and promoting them into leadership roles. The best teacher in each grade level serves as a lead teacher, who leads weekly PD meetings. Is this essentially the same idea?*

**Answer:** We believe there is a fundamental difference in our approach to identifying and developing school leadership. Our goal is not to identify the "best" teachers and move them into leadership positions. We believe true leadership development requires a different mindset and a different (but overlapping) set of skills. Certainly, most schools already have systems in place that identify the best teachers—which might be determined by test results, student behavior, classroom observations and ratings, or informal methods. Our view, however, is that these strategies might identify successful teachers, but they might still fail to identify and develop the skills and mindsets that are required for instructional leadership.

In this book, we suggest a school structure that deliberately places all teachers in a system that demands intensive collaboration around teaching. As a result, this collaborative process—which includes lesson planning, collaboration, and teaching—helps identify this broader range of skills that demonstrate leadership capacity. In other words, the system we describe in the chapters that follow is deliberately designed to identify and develop a broader range of skills than those just identified with classroom teaching.

# 3

## Collaboration in the Artisan Teaching Model

The Artisan Teaching system seeks to provide all support for teachers within a single, comprehensive system of collaboration within a team. Later in this chapter, we will detail how we have implemented this approach at AMS. But first, it is important to understand the rationale and objective behind key features of the system.

## The Principles Underlying the Artisan Teaching Approach

To implement a collaborative model successfully, to support these systems with all necessary resources, and to find new and creative ways to make it work within your own school, you first must grasp its underlying philosophy. Without this foundation, it will be difficult if not impossible to develop a consistent approach.

> **Artisan Teaching Principle 1:** The focus of this team is the development, design, delivery, and critique of daily lessons. This is the primary work product of collaborative teams, because this is the work that matters most to the people producing it.

Although most schools engage teachers in a wide range of work involving various types of collaborative teams, the Artisan Teaching system focuses on teams that teach the same course to the same grade and share a curriculum. This point is crucial when considering how to design the makeup of the collaborative teams that are central to the model.

Granted, we believe there is value in meetings of other collaborative groups—including grade-level "kid talk" teams to discuss the needs of at-risk children across disciplines and "vertical planning teams" that meet to align curriculum in one subject area across grade levels. But one of the core philosophical underpinnings of the Artisan Teaching system is that the actual day-to-day work teachers do (i.e., lesson planning and instruction) and the frustration that goes along with this day-to-day work is most important and most often experienced alone. The Artisan Teaching system addresses this isolation through the deliberate formulation of teams at the grade/subject level.

With this organizational need in mind, the Artisan Teaching system lends itself naturally to secondary schools with more than 150 students at each grade level. These schools typically must have more than one teacher in each subject area at each grade level. (Assuming a maximum teaching assignment of five classes of 30 kids each, one teacher generally cannot teach more than 150 students.) For smaller schools, however, it is customary to assign one teacher to teach all of the students in one grade in the teacher's subject area. For example, these schools generally have one 9th grade English teacher, one 10th grade math teacher, one 11th grade history teacher, and so forth. These schools often were deliberately designed to create small learning communities for students, based on research demonstrating that approximately 100 students in each grade maximizes a sense of community in the school. This model, however, fails to consider the appropriate learning community for *teachers*. Teachers are typically assigned to be a "team of one" with respect to their teaching assignments. The result of isolating teachers in their most important work can be an efficient system to administer, but it also can have truly brutal effects on the psyche of a teacher, who is largely left to do his or her most important work alone.

Although it is tempting to do so, school leaders should not assign one teacher to teach all students in the grade. The Artisan Teaching system requires the architects of small schools to organize their teaching assignments with deliberate, purposeful inefficiency in order to create adult learning communities around the most important work. We have found several ways to structure teaching assignments to allow the Artisan Teaching system to work, even with only 85 students at each grade level. (See Chapter 6 for small-school implementation strategies.)

> **Artisan Teaching Principle 2:** The most effective environment for the development of great teachers is one in which individuals work in collegial teams that are jointly responsible for successful student outcomes.

The Artisan Teaching model creates a group dynamic that is positive and supportive and that requires teachers to work together toward a joint objective. The work of the team is intentionally frequent and wide-ranging, providing both daily accountability to a team and also a supportive, collegial environment. When one teacher on a team presents a new idea for a lesson, it is in the interest of the other team members to listen, provide feedback that might improve the idea, and decide (collectively) whether to implement it in all classrooms. Participants are almost always on task because the topic—usually how to teach the next day's lesson—is timely and highly relevant to everyone at the meeting. Feedback from within the team is most often genuine and relevant because the team consists only of teachers sharing the same course every day.

> **Artisan Teaching Principle 3:** The most effective model of support and development for professionals in any field is one of collaboration with experts.

New members of virtually every profession are paired with more experienced and successful members of the profession to work together on a daily basis—often for their entire careers. Doctors work as residents for four years before becoming fully licensed to practice; their residencies serve as apprenticeships with more experienced doctors. Newer doctors observe and work together with those veterans during the work with patients. Police officers work with partners, serving together in a single car. They support and learn from each other while doing the work of their profession. Airplanes have two pilots. Accountants and lawyers work on audits and briefs in teams; younger team members write drafts and veterans edit the final work that goes to the client or judge.

The Artisan Teaching system assumes that teaching is as important as any other profession and therefore deserves the same level of respect for its professionals and their craft. Teachers deserve the support of other teachers working jointly toward a common goal on a daily basis—engaging in the work together before they teach their lessons, and not merely receiving occasional advice or ratings from a supervisor after the lesson has been delivered. Just as in every other profession, collaboration is the best way to develop and improve the work of individuals. Moreover, our children also deserve a curriculum and lessons that have been prepared by a team—just as a patient in a hospital deserves treatment that is being devised by more than one doctor, and just as a passenger deserves service from an airline with more than one pilot flying the plane.

> **Artisan Teaching Principle** 4: Support for teachers within a
> school is best provided in a singular system rather than through
> a variety of overlapping systems and supports for each teacher.

Consider a 7th grade classroom in which Johnnie throws a pencil across Ms. Smith's room during a mathematics lesson. The Artisan Teaching system is based in part on a belief that Johnnie's misbehavior is most effectively addressed—and Ms. Smith is best supported—collaboratively with a Team Leader. Only the Team Leader for the 7th grade math classes (along with Ms. Smith) will have all of the information necessary to address the situation. *Why did Johnnie throw the pencil? Was the math lesson too difficult? Does Johnnie struggle in Ms. Smith's class? Was the lesson too boring? Was Ms. Smith's lesson too long—and was that when Johnnie threw the pencil? Did he throw the pencil during a test, during a group project, or during silent work? Is behavior a common problem in that class? Does Ms. Smith have behavior problems during her other classes? Has the team been discussing classroom management strategies? Would PD be worthwhile for Ms. Smith? Could Ms. Smith prevent a repetition of this incident by scaffolding assignments differently? Or by cold calling to keep all students more engaged? Or by implementing a new seating chart? Or by considering a new special-ed strategy?* A real solution to this problem must incorporate all of this information—most of which relates to the lesson planning, instruction, and professional development of Ms. Smith. If schools address these issues in isolation (e.g., just punish Johnnie), then they fail to address the underlying cause of the problem and fail to take the necessary steps to help prevent the issue from recurring.

The Artisan Teaching model is aimed squarely at addressing the "overlapping" nature of issues that arise in schools. Discipline issues involve instruction, classroom management techniques, relationships, data, and so forth. Therefore, all of these issues must be discussed collaboratively by the teacher and one person (the TL), in order to provide a real solution that addresses the root of the problem.

---

**DIARY OF A TEACHER**
**Artisan Teaching Team Meeting (November)**

*"This is bad. Kids are not listening to me," I said at my team meeting today. "Maybe these kids just can't do this." My teammates reminded me of the walk we took last month where I saw the same kids completely on task. "Maybe the dean could come in and just get them settled," I tried. Another screeching halt. Johnson said that kids would see this as weak. "You do that and it'll really send it over the edge. Kids will see that you doubt yourself, and 7th graders, especially, are built to detect this." They told me that now, the low point, is precisely when I need to stay consistent—continue to call home, stop talking over kids, make key relationships, narrate good behavior—and in doing so, it will turn around.*

*"Remember," Rodriguez said, "This is a career you are building. It takes consistency, humility, and time. We expected that you would have trouble—that is normal. We have the patience for you to learn, but the question is, do you?" Rodriguez said she will come*

*in tomorrow, not to intervene but to do another whole-class obser-vation and give me tips afterward.*

Indeed, educators agree that most important issues arising in schools relate to the quality of instruction. It is inconsistent with this philosophy for schools to assign one administrator to address discipline issues, a data specialist to conduct schoolwide data analysis, a coach to support lesson planning across grade levels, an assistant principal to lead school-wide PD sessions, a principal to provide monthly observation feedback, and a mentor to provide advice for first-year teachers. All of these sup-ports are necessarily disjointed, and all of the school officials will lack necessary information to solve problems in a comprehensive way. By merging all of these roles into one, comprehensive system, the Artisan Teaching model provides support that is qualitatively different.

### DIARY OF A TEACHER
### Artisan Teaching Team Meeting—
### Data Analysis Meeting (March)

*During our meeting today, we were looking at the student answers from our recent exam. As we went through the exams, it was clear that Johnson's students did much better than mine. Each set of student answers became another opportunity for me to learn. We taught the same lesson plans, but why were Johnson's kids con-sistently doing better? To be sure, part had to do with my class-room management, which for most of the year was rough. But in talking with Johnson, there were choices made, differences in what he stressed. What were those choices, and why did he make them? What should I do differently? Though we needed the data for this conversation, the conversation wasn't really about data; the con-versation was about me.*

**Artisan Teaching Principle 5:** Teachers overwhelmingly benefit the most from professional development that is delivered in
small groups, tailored to the individual needs of each teacher and
grounded in the teacher's day-to-day planning.

The Artisan Teaching system is a transformation of traditional professional development. The goal of the Artisan Teaching model is to provide a time and space for experts to work together on a day-to-day basis
with less-experienced teachers on all of the most important work that
teaching requires. In doing so, the collaborative work renders superfluous many of the professional development sessions that schools typically provide.

For example, when a TL works with a team on lesson planning
every day, there is no need to conduct workshops on lesson planning
during PD time after school. When a TL works with teachers to incorporate differentiation strategies into their joint lesson plans every day,
there is no need for a schoolwide initiative to improve differentiation
of instruction. And when the TLs are responsible for working with their
teams on discipline issues whenever they arise, there is little purpose
in a series of classroom management training sessions at the school
level. The school leaders' role in providing professional development
for teachers is the most fundamental role of instructional leadership—
but the Artisan Teaching model creates a new mindset about that role.
PD is provided more effectively in small teams, where it is delivered in
context and tailored to the individual needs of each teacher; in doing
so, other school PD structures become unnecessary (see Figures 3.1
and 3.2).

**Artisan Teaching Principle 6:** The Artisan Teaching system prizes
curriculum development as a necessary component of developing artisans, with many parallels to the system of "Japanese lesson study."

Schools and school districts in the United States employ a wildly
diverse range of systems for curriculum development, ranging from
complete autonomy (where schools allow and require teachers to write

every lesson from scratch with little guidance) to no autonomy at all (where teachers are required to follow word-by-word scripts of the lessons they must teach). Most schools use a system somewhere between these two extremes, in which teachers receive textbooks and state standards that students must learn, but they are left to plan the daily activities themselves (as long as the students are prepared for the assessments at the end of the year).

As we have discussed, the Artisan Teaching model is based primarily on a philosophy of adult development, designed to improve the work of

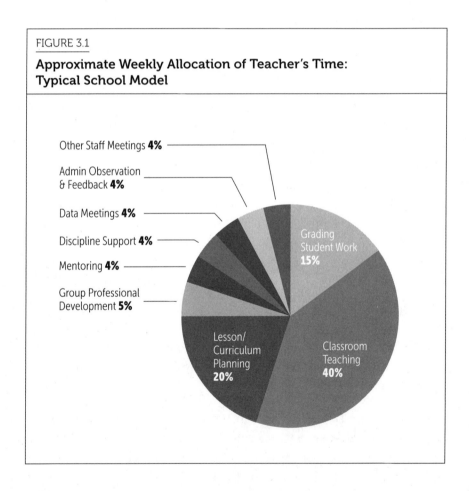

FIGURE 3.1

**Approximate Weekly Allocation of Teacher's Time: Typical School Model**

teachers and instructional leaders. Nevertheless, the same features of the Artisan Teaching model that serve to develop higher-quality instruction also serve another purpose: to create an effective and sustainable system of curriculum development within the school. The collaborative team process results in a fully written curriculum, with unit plans and daily lessons that were taught by a team of teachers in all of the classes. That curriculum is co-planned, taught, and debriefed by a team throughout the year; then the curriculum is saved for the following year for the team to reuse, edit, or modify.

FIGURE 3.2

**Approximate Weekly Allocation of Teacher's Time: Artisan Teaching Model**

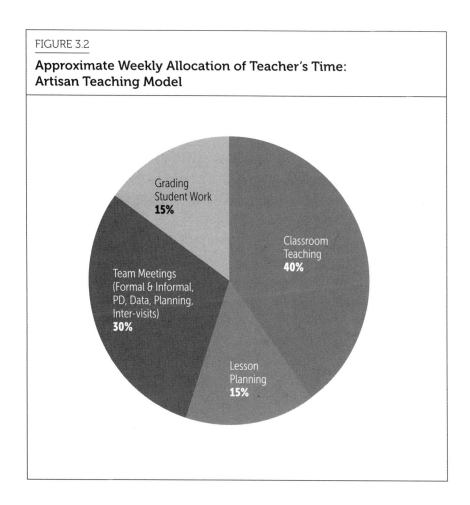

The result is a balanced approach to curriculum development with many benefits to the teachers and the school: (1) all teachers have the freedom to write lessons from scratch or to edit lessons and add new ideas, without a mandated textbook or script (limited only by the requirement that they collaborate and reach consensus with their colleagues and TL); (2) teachers have a curriculum available to them from the previous school year that is consistent with the school philosophy, and they are not left without support (especially important for newer teachers); and (3) the collaborative process leads to constant review and revision of school lessons, with an ever-improving school curriculum that always has the benefit of new ideas whenever new teachers join a team. This model provides freedom for teacher creativity as well as accountability from the team for high-quality lesson planning. It provides a school curriculum with prewritten materials that most new teachers appreciate but no scripts or mandates that limit a teacher's ownership and input.

The Artisan Teaching system, therefore, holds many similarities to the model of Japanese lesson study, where teams of teachers meticulously analyze a day's lesson, observe the delivery of the lesson, debrief the results, and repeatedly edit the lesson to improve the results. The lesson study model aims to create a continually improving lesson that is passed along from one year to the next, always improving after each group's revision. The Artisan Teaching system provides many of the same results.

> **Artisan Teaching Principle 7:** Leadership development should start for teachers as early as possible in their careers, and teachers from the outset should be simultaneously learning to teach and to lead.

We believe that teachers' attitudes about leadership start to form as soon as they are led; therefore, it makes great sense to influence a leadership disposition from the outset. We believe it is just too late to start leadership discussions and leadership training activities after the teacher has formed an understanding of the teaching profession. Future leaders need to feel that part of becoming a great teacher is exerting the discipline and fortitude necessary to develop a strong internal locus of control. The work involved in developing a strong internal locus of control—in yourself or in others—lies at the heart of leadership development. In fact, if a teacher forms the right habits of mind as a teacher, then the initial shift to leadership depends more on an affinity for leadership than on an ability for leadership.

The quest to make an outstanding leader out of anybody with potential begs the question: *How does a school make sure that none of these potential leaders falls through the cracks?* The school needs a vehicle, led by someone who can spot and develop leadership, by which leaders can use authentic, difficult situations to engender a growth mindset.

**Artisan Teaching Principle 8:** The unification of all of the important work into one structure is necessary for the internal generation of leaders.

A leadership vehicle needs to feature a contained system (rather than provide a variety of outlets for difficulties). For example, by forcing discipline issues to be handled at the team level, the TL can expertly link most student misbehavior correctly to a pedagogical deficiency—something the teacher needs to and can improve upon. It is unfair and unrealistic to expect a dean to understand all of the nuances in instruction and student behavior across all subjects and grade levels in order to lead just the right teacher conversation in just the right way so the teacher will learn to see the issue as one of teacher growth rather than student misbehavior. In an overlapping system, for example, where the dean handles all student misbehavior, the TL is denied the opportunity to be a better developer of leaders. The TL needs these authentic challenges to arise so he or she can develop leaders through them. A leadership vehicle must be small enough to be nimbly and artfully led, must be authentic to all participants, must be collaborative in nature, and must have mutual accountability.

## The Artisan Teaching Model in Action

In this section, we detail the features of the model as it has been implemented at AMS—not as a blueprint to be copied but as a foundational example that can be referenced in creating your own team model of Artisan Teaching.

## Core Features

- *Team makeup:* The team consists of two or more teachers who teach the same course to similar groups of students in the same grade level. One of those teachers (or an additional team member) is a highly successful artisan teacher or administrator who has taught the course before and who meets the qualifications to serve as a Team Leader.
- *Team meetings:* The members of the team meet on a regular basis, both formally and informally. They have at least two weekly, formal, regularly scheduled meetings built into their official work schedules. These meetings last for at least one class period (i.e., at least one hour).
- *Team leader role:* In many ways, these are the key assignments for the school. Some TLs are school administrators and some are artisan teachers, but all are given adequate time both to support the team and to receive support from the administrators. If the TL is a teacher, he or she is provided with a reduced teaching assignment allowing approximately one additional "prep" period for each team the TL leads. This extra period, free from classroom instruction, is used to provide additional supports for his or her teammates (described further later in this chapter) and also to meet regularly with the other TLs and school leaders. To enable frequent classroom visits, the TL also must have a "prep" period during at least one period when each of his or her teammates teaches the shared course.
- *Shared curriculum and lesson planning:* The members of the team coplan, share, and teach the same lesson plan on a daily basis.

The calendar, assignments, assessments, and grading scales are the same for all sections of the course. The curriculum is developed, written, and edited jointly by all members of the team.

- *New teacher support:* The TL serves as the "new teacher mentor" for any first- or second-year teachers on the team. Advice, mentoring, and training for new teachers are delivered by the TL through the system, and no additional (formal) mentoring structures are needed.

- *Professional development:* The TL serves as the primary facilitator of professional development for the teachers on the team. The TL is responsible for assessing each teacher's professional needs and for planning developmental work to help each teacher improve. The TL provides individualized PD for each team member through the team's formal and informal meetings, which feature the highest-leveraged on-the-job adult development activities: writing lesson plans, modeling high-quality instruction, making classroom visits with debriefs, conducting preteach rehearsals, and role-playing classroom management. There are rarely any full-faculty PD sessions. In fact, few PD activities have more than four people in attendance since, in the Artisan Teaching system, there are at most four people with the same shared teaching experience. This is, for us, a critical condition for creating authentic and deep adult learning about the craft of teaching.

- *Classroom observations and feedback:* The TL is responsible for providing the other team members with routine classroom observations and feedback. These visits vary in frequency and duration, depending on the experience and needs of the teachers, but the focus is on very high-frequency, unscheduled visits. These visits take place at least twice a week; for developing teachers, they occur daily. During these visits, the TL provides feedback for the teacher, considers PD needs, checks for student achievement, and monitors consistency of student learning in the various sections of the course across the grade level.

- *Data analysis:* The collaborative teams are responsible for monitoring and analyzing student data for their subject/grade. They share collective responsibility for understanding student progress across the grade level, identifying and supporting at-risk students, and considering strategies for addressing gaps in student learning.

- *Discipline support:* The collaborative teams are responsible for discussing discipline issues occurring within any of the classrooms on their team. The TL provides the primary support for teachers struggling with classroom management issues. Although there are schoolwide discipline structures (mostly for out-of-classroom issues and for offenses involving bias or violence), the TL pushes back on all routine classroom discipline and works with the teacher to identify root causes that almost always link back to teacher actions or inactions and that provide opportunity for teacher growth.

- *Students with disabilities:* The collaborative teams also serve as the primary point of contact for the teachers providing services for students with disabilities and English language learners within that grade/subject. We try to staff every collaborative team with at least one teacher responsible for students with disabilities, thereby allowing seamless inclusion of special education strategies into all daily lesson plans (and guaranteeing ample time for collaboration among general education and special education teachers throughout the school, within the team framework).

- *Support for TLs:* Leading adults formally for the first time can be quite a shock to the new leader, and the Artisan Teaching system also includes critical support and development of Team Leaders. The TLs meet regularly and often to learn from one another about leading adults, and they also meet with an administrator (assistant principal or principal) several times per week, as needed. These meetings are in-context, real-time analyses of the TL's work with teachers. First-year TLs usually meet several hours a week with an administrator; veteran TLs, less.

## Additional Features

Of course, programming and scheduling realities make it difficult to incorporate *every* strategy into *every* team's day—especially when being mindful of how busy and intense a teacher's workday already is. Nevertheless, as many of the following additional features should be included as often as possible:

- *Strategic prep periods:* The TL and teacher prep periods should be used strategically to increase teacher interaction. For example, a first-year teacher might be assigned a prep during first period, allowing him to observe the TL teach the lesson every day. Next, the new teacher could teach the same lesson (to his own classes) during second and fourth periods. During fourth period, the TL is assigned a prep, allowing her to observe the new teacher. Finally, they might have a common prep during sixth period (when team meetings occur), allowing an opportunity to debrief the day.

- *Shared classrooms:* The TL and a newer member of the team should share a classroom, which can be used for both of their sections of the same course throughout the day. By teaching all sections of the same course in the same room, the teammates share a collegial space where they can also share instructional techniques and classroom routines (e.g., spacing, room design, entry procedures). This promotes greater collegiality and increases opportunities for informal communication and classroom observations.

- *Team teaching:* Depending on the school's schedules and special education rules, the TL could coteach one section of the course with a teammate. If one teacher is licensed in a content area and another is licensed in special education, this form of team teaching can be facilitated by using a collaborative teaching or push-in support model for students whose IEPs mandate that support. This provides yet another opportunity for shared responsibility among members of the collaborative team.

## Chapter 3

**Question:** *It sounds like you are suggesting that all teachers* must *share daily lesson plans. What happens in the Artisan Teaching model if a teacher does not want to share lessons every day?*

**Answer:** The reality in the Artisan Teaching model is that the sharing of lessons naturally results without any need for mandate. If teachers enjoy collaboration and see the value in working together as part of a team, the benefits of sharing lessons are immediately obvious: they have a partner giving daily feedback and suggestions, and they develop better lessons as a result.

At AMS, we have never had a new teacher question the lesson-sharing system. The benefits and support from the system are obvious, and the new teachers uniformly praise the opportunity to share lessons. For veteran teachers, the sharing of lessons is similarly beneficial to those who share a similar view of teaching with the school leaders. If they appreciate the quality of the shared lessons and feedback from Team Leaders, then they do not dispute the benefits of the system—and they are generally excited to serve in a mentoring role, supporting the newer teachers on their teams. Veteran teachers are proud and validated to see their lesson ideas have a positive effect on the entire school, and they appreciate the assistance of their teammates in writing new lessons.

Occasionally, a teacher expresses displeasure with the shared lesson planning system because that teacher's views about instruction (and the lessons he or she is writing and delivering) are inconsistent with the school's mission. When that "conflict" arises, a teacher may express a desire to plan individually without the support or collaboration with colleagues and Team Leaders. This must be addressed—not ignored and hidden by allowing the teacher to continue teaching with an instructional philosophy that is different from the school's. The disagreements that arise when a teacher doesn't want to share lessons every day, in other words, are disagreements that must be resolved openly. If the answer is for teachers to continue planning lessons alone, because they don't see eye to eye, then the school's instructional mission will be compromised, with or without the Artisan Teaching approach.

# 4

The Effects of the
Artisan Teaching System

The results of the schoolwide Artisan Teaching system at AMS have been strong, consistent over the long term, and multifaceted. Some outcomes might be expected or even obvious; others are less predictable.

## Culture of Teaching and Learning

It is clear at AMS that teachers and leaders enjoy and value discussing pedagogy. Teachers are constantly talking about lessons and verbalizing the ups and downs of their daily instruction. Of course, they are required to talk about lessons in their scheduled team meetings, but over time, it becomes much deeper than that. At a school that requires its entire staff to meet and collaborate on lesson planning and instruction every day, a culture of reflectiveness and a growth mindset naturally follows. Teachers are hired because they enjoy discussing ways to improve instruction, and they meet every day to do so. They visit one another's classrooms every day to share ways to improve instruction; when new teachers are frustrated and experience behavior problems, the school leaders continue pushing them to consider how to improve their instruction. Even schoolwide data analysis and PD initiatives are largely replaced by additional opportunities for small groups of teachers to work independently on the improvement of their own curriculum and instruction.

---

**DIARY OF A TEACHER**
**Subway Conversation (December)**

*Everywhere I turn—in a stairwell, at the coffee machine—everyone seems to be talking about instruction. Today, on the subway, I ran into a Team Leader from another grade who asked me, "Did you do anything cool today to make kids think?" I had to think about it for a few minutes. "Today's lesson about equations was a bit boring for the kids, but they loved the project on Monday and Tuesday about the T-shirt sale. The kids had to make a business plan, and they really got into it." The Team Leader asked, "Why do you think they liked it?"*

---

Virtually every aspect of the apprenticeship system pushes teachers to talk more, again and again, about their lessons and instruction. The overwhelming sentiment of Artisan Teaching staff is that good teaching produces good results, and that good teaching is a difficult craft that takes many years to develop. Teachers are proud of good lessons because they spent time writing and planning them, and they take ownership of the results because they know their students will benefit from their hard work. The systematic focus on teacher collaboration around their curriculum and lesson plans creates a culture that elevates and respects the craft of teaching. Teaching deserves that respect and attention to detail, and the daily discussion with experts is the way to make it happen.

## Student Success

The Artisan Teaching system has led to strong and consistent long-term student achievement results at AMS. This outcome might be somewhat surprising, since the school philosophy has never focused heavily on test prep or data analysis. For over 10 years, the administration has rarely discussed test score results with individual teachers or teams, rarely suggested or mandated pre-tests or interim assessments throughout the school year, and focused its after-school and summer programming on enrichment (mostly sports, hiking and camping trips, the arts, and keeping kids reading), not test prep.

Like school leaders everywhere, we understand the political and pedagogical importance of achievement results—we want to make sure our students are learning, and we want people to know that they are. We do not, however, think that a constant focus on test scores is the way to make that happen. No banners in the hallway count down the days until the Big Test. No bulletin boards fill up with bar charts and graphs detailing the latest disaggregated performance on state exams. All that hoopla around the Big Test, we believe, makes adults feel like they are creating urgency around test scores, when in fact all they are doing is creating *anxiety* for everyone: teachers, parents, and students. We are aware of no research to support the idea that kids do better when a school publicly counts down to test day. All the common sense in the world suggests that this would create anxiety among those who struggle most—for example, the 70 percent of kids in New York City who are below grade level. We feel particular sympathy for kids who fear testing and are bombarded with countdown signs. And we feel for kids who struggle with standardized test performance and who must daily pass by bulletin boards boasting recent schoolwide achievement—not to mention the pretests, interim assessments, and practice tests within the classroom. This is the data movement gone too far. Adults should pour all of that energy into writing better lessons and learning to deliver them more effectively.

There is very legitimate work around testing. We have our teams analyze and discuss the requirements of the New York State exams, and we understand that we are held accountable for our students' scores on those exams. But the idea of getting students pumped for a test is antithetical to our belief in school. Students should get pumped up about *learning*, not standardized measures. We believe that the shared curriculum and collaborative work of teacher teams virtually guarantees improvement in student achievement.

Regardless of one's views on testing, our school shows that a focus on the depth and rigor of instructional practice through collaboration will yield the right results for children. If a school successfully focuses on the quality of teaching, the results should be apparent by any well-designed measure. On state assessments, AMS has achieved consistently strong results over the course of a decade. Specifically, New York City rates all schools using two data-based metrics: the Progress Report (based on annual data from New York State standardized assessments) and the Quality Review (a rubric-based assessment of the school's instruction and other practices). AMS has earned the highest possible ratings ("A," "B," and "Well Developed") in every year's ratings since the school was founded.

On metrics of deeper learning, AMS has one of the highest rates of "college readiness" of any nonscreened public school in New York City. It also has an extremely low rate of major disciplinary incidents, an 85 percent articulation rate of 8th graders choosing to remain at the school for high school, a 90 percent historical on-time graduation rate (see Figure 4.1), over 80 percent on-time graduation for students with disabilities, and one of the highest rates of college matriculation of any nonscreened school in New York City (see Figure 4.2).

Recent research suggests that some of the most important indicators of student achievement may include social-emotional health and development of life skills such as perseverance and grit. Although these characteristics are challenging to measure, we believe they result naturally from higher-quality teaching that focuses on the long-term development of students. The Artisan Teaching collaborative apprenticeship system results in a built-in sense of rigor and accountability (to the students and to one's team), and the result is extraordinarily consistent long-term student success. When new teachers finish their second year at AMS, they appear to be achieving higher rates of student success than teachers of similar experience at other schools (where they are not supported by a common planning partner and Team Leader). When a teacher leaves AMS, the work of that teacher to improve the curriculum is not lost (because the planning partner passes along the benefit of the collaboration the following year). All students benefit from a common and consistent instructional philosophy that the collaborative system fosters.

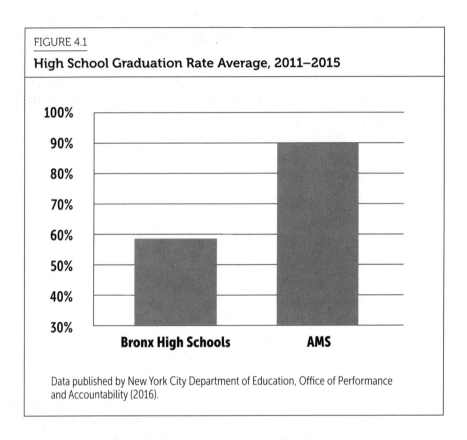

FIGURE 4.1

**High School Graduation Rate Average, 2011–2015**

Data published by New York City Department of Education, Office of Performance and Accountability (2016).

## Teacher Development

One of the most powerful benefits of the Artisan Teaching system is its impact on teachers who are new to the profession. The apprenticeship model results in a far more comprehensive and intensive level of support for first-year teachers than most schools offer. Indeed, it is a new model for first-year teacher training that stands in contrast to the disjointed, inconsistent support that many schools provide for new teachers, where

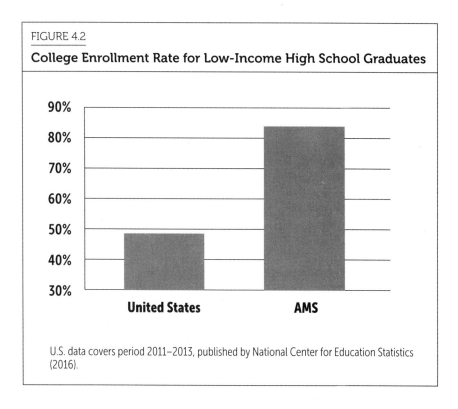

FIGURE 4.2

**College Enrollment Rate for Low-Income High School Graduates**

U.S. data covers period 2011–2013, published by National Center for Education Statistics (2016).

a mentor speaks with them (once a month), an administrator observes them (once a month), a coach provides PD (once a week), and a dean or assistant principal helps with discipline (only *after* a problem occurs). The Artisan Teaching apprenticeship model merges all of these supports into one, comprehensive model of support that greatly improves the rate of success and pace of development of new teachers.

AMS has embraced its role in training new teachers in New York City. While some schools seek to avoid this job entirely, making it a practice to hire only veterans, AMS relishes the energy and talent of brand-new teachers and has continued hiring some first-year teachers every year. We are proud to do so, because we believe our school is well designed to support new teachers by partnering them with expert veterans. Admittedly, we often have little choice, because it is difficult to hire successful veteran teachers in a low-income community such as ours. Regardless of the reason, we do not think our students would be succeeding at such high rates with this number of new and inexperienced teachers if not for the collaborative system that helps those new teachers develop so quickly.

## Leaders Focus on What Matters Most

One of the most important and common concerns expressed by school leaders is how they are pulled in so many different directions—with so many job requirements that they are left with no time for the work that matters most: supporting instruction. Another result of the Artisan Teaching system is the streamlining of so many leadership roles into one, coherent leadership structure that minimizes the time devoted to these other leadership demands. We believe the system of daily instructional collaboration described in this book greatly alleviates these concerns. The Artisan Teaching model requires a huge devotion of effort, time, and resources—but the results are incredibly liberating for the school leaders.

What are the systematic issues that arise so often and pull school leaders from their focus on instruction?

- *Discipline:* In the Artisan Teaching system, the first step when discipline issues arise is for the leader to push back on a request for disciplinary support. The first step must be for the team to consider the instructional or child development problem that is causing misbehavior, and to push the team to take ownership of the problem and develop a solution. TLs are experienced and equipped to provide that support. Indeed, it is not that the team system allows leaders to avoid the work; rather, it is a philosophical underpinning of the system that the problem will be addressed more effectively by focusing on the classroom. And this is the role of the team, not the principal, assistant principal, or dean.

- *Professional development:* In the Artisan Teaching system, the first step is *not* to provide schoolwide PD sessions focusing on a schoolwide objective that is planned and coordinated by school leaders. Rather, Team Leaders are qualified and equipped to assess the needs of the individual teachers on their teams, and they should choose those areas of professional development for (and with) each teacher. The burden of choosing and planning schoolwide PD initiatives is less important, and the school leader rests confident that the most effective PD is occurring in the team meetings every day.

- *Data analysis:* In many schools, leaders are organizing and compiling achievement data on a routine basis. In the Artisan Teaching system, the leaders spend very little time doing so. We prefer the TLs to spend most of their time working with teachers on lessons and instruction, not data analysis, because the TLs will have an intimate understanding of the student achievement by virtue of their own observations and presence in the classrooms every day. While a school principal may need to conduct reviews of spreadsheets to quickly assess the student learning in 20, 30, or 50 classrooms, the team system creates a new model of distributed leadership that renders the spreadsheets superfluous. If the principal knows that the TLs share the principal's view of rigor and achievement, the principal can rest assured that the TL will analyze data when needed. Schoolwide data analysis becomes largely unnecessary, because it would merely serve to corroborate what the Team Leaders already know.

In short, the Artisan Teaching apprenticeship model creates a huge shift in the role of the school leader, by empowering a group of emerging instructional leaders (the Team Leaders) to serve as the "proxies" for the leader's instructional vision. And by centralizing nearly all of the school's structures and supports for teachers within that single system of distributed instructional leaders (in the teams and team meetings), many of the so-called distractions that burden the school leader are eliminated. And what do the AMS principals and assistant principals do with that extra time that is available, now that so many of the functions of the other roles are being filled by Team Leaders? They serve as Team Leaders themselves.

## A Balanced Model for School Curriculum Development

Another result of the Artisan Teaching model is a continually improving *school curriculum*. Since its inception, AMS has not mandated any specific textbooks or scripted curriculum for its teachers, but after a decade of common planning, a school curriculum exists and is passed along to the next year's teachers to edit, refine, improve, or rewrite completely. Every year, a teacher may have a new idea for a project or essay or might rewrite the lessons with a different style or voice. But lessons are consistent with the school's overall mission focusing on student engagement and real-life applications, and they are discussed in every situation with a Team Leader. The result is loosely analogous to the Japanese lesson study model, where a lesson is repeatedly taught, analyzed, and revised in an effort to continually improve it—until the lesson is truly great (see Artisan Teaching Principle 6 in Chapter 3). At AMS, the curriculum in different grades and subjects is always a work in progress, always waiting for another team to improve it. But one of the benefits of the system is that the curriculum exists—a remnant of the collaborative work the teachers do this year and a resource for the collaborative teams in years that follow.

Indeed, we suggest that the Artisan Teaching model provides a flexible approach for schoolwide curriculum development, because it naturally adjusts for the needs of all teachers within the school—regardless of their level of experience. In this system, all teachers are provided with a clear vision of the school's beliefs about instruction. All teachers have ample opportunity for input into every day's lesson, and creativity and innovation are encouraged. The curriculum is neither static nor scripted. But for newer teachers who are burdened by excessive responsibilities of the new profession, the Artisan Teaching apprenticeship provides huge support as well—a fully written curriculum that is shared by the team. It allows some teachers to use the apprenticeship to get more support (acting more as the "apprentice") and, simultaneously, allows other teachers to engage more actively with their teams in a role that fosters creative, innovative curriculum design. Both are achieved within the same system—and the only requirement is that teachers complete this work within the team structure.

## Sustainability

We have all heard many stories of schools enjoying early success only to have results drop due to the departure of a founding principal or of other key personnel. Other common threats to continued long-term success include fluctuating funding levels, lack of available excellent teachers and excellent leaders to hire from the outside, and systemic leadership changes. AMS has overcome all of these pitfalls and increased student achievement because what holds the enterprise together transcends any one leader, inside or outside the school: an unwavering belief in the power of—and the duty to become—an artisan teacher. The permeation of this vision, and ultimately the sustainability of the school, derives almost exclusively from the robust and deeply ingrained Artisan Teaching structure. The structure allows leaders to deeply invest in and honor adults. The structure allows leaders to generate the next wave of leaders. The structure allows leaders to preserve both student and adult culture.

**Chapter 4**

**Question:** *It sounds like you are suggesting that schools using the Artisan Teaching approach will need to eliminate whole-school PD sessions, data analysis meetings, and other departmental meetings suggested or required by my district. How can a school implement this model and remain true to the district vision?*

**Answer:** We believe the Artisan Teaching model can be implemented while meeting all city or district mandates. AMS is a public school in New York City, and we have never found our structure to be inconsistent with city rules in any way. The Artisan Teaching approach provides all of the same supports that school districts require but reorganizes the work in a new way. We provide PD; we provide new teacher mentoring; we conduct classroom observations and feedback cycles; and we analyze data. We choose to merge all of these supports into a single small-group structure with one Team Leader, instead of providing each support from a different school leader in a series of separate weekly meetings.

Indeed, in addition to increasing student achievement, part of many districts' rationales around teacher meetings is to foster *adult community* with professional, productive relationships, and that is precisely what the Artisan Teaching system is engineered to do. In fact, if collegial bonds are part of a district vision, then the working relationships forged in the team structure will most likely be stronger than those built via the traditional structures because of the joint accountability of the work product that the Artisan Teaching system demands.

**Question:** *It sounds like you are criticizing the two most commonly used systems for improving classroom instruction: professional development meetings and observation/feedback cycles. Are you really suggesting that these two cornerstones of teacher development are ineffective?*

**Answer:** We believe these two structures are failing to improve classroom instruction at the rate that is necessary to improve a school. Of course, these systems provide *some* benefit, and *some* teachers will improve using the current systems. And of course, we believe that teachers need observations, feedback, and professional development. But the core belief described in this book is that schools have mistakenly separated teacher evaluation and professional development from the real, day-to-day work that teachers do. The educational community has (erroneously, in our opinion) created a series of separate structures, each led by a different school leader, which is minimizing their overall impact.

Classroom observations and feedback are crucial, but they are dramatically more impactful when they are performed by a Team Leader who is collaborating with the teacher on a daily basis on lesson planning, classroom routines, discipline, differentiation of instruction, and everything else. When classroom observations are done by an administrator whose only view of the classroom is an occasional visit, the impact is minimal.

Similarly, professional development is crucial—but it is dramatically more impactful when it is provided in context by a Team Leader who is collaborating with that teacher on all daily work. When PD sessions are add-ons at the end of the day, separated from the lessons and units that the teachers are working on that day, the benefits are so diluted as to render them almost moot.

**Question:** *The Artisan Teaching model seems to contradict the vision of "data-driven instruction." Do you support the data movement in education?*

**Answer:** No. Perhaps the one true inconsistency between the Artisan Teaching model and current trends in education reform and many district mandates is around data-driven instruction. There is no getting around the fact that the Artisan Teaching model does not feature teachers poring over exit slips or giving much attention to item-analysis data from standardized tests. We do not believe that is how teachers should be spending their time. Some educators point out that great teachers are *always* looking informally at "data"—by reading their students' writing and assessing their conceptual understandings. But our view is that the data trend in education has become obsessed with numerical data analysis (and more specifically, test results) as a substitute for these types of authentic, in-the-moment student assessment. To the contrary, we believe a laserlike focus on great teaching will result in great achievement data—*and not the other way around.*

# 5

## The Leadership Pipeline

Trying to hire external school leaders is a brutal prospect. Superintendents and principals know this well. On a grand scale, large cities have over the years invested heavily in recruiting leaders nationally but have been largely unable to do so. The point here is not to do a critique of these efforts but, on the contrary, highlight just how difficult (or even impossible) a task external leadership recruitment is in the school context.

First, the pool of high-quality leaders who are willing to move schools is a small pool indeed. Successful leaders usually like their jobs, enjoy their professional relationships, and most often see leadership advancement at their current locations. They often already have what they want. Giving up that security for the unknown is unlikely. Second, public schools funded essentially on tax levy monies do not have the resources to get into bidding wars with each other. Third, it is really difficult to tell if an external leadership candidate is an effective leader—way harder than discerning if an external teaching candidate is an effective teacher.

Candidates for teaching jobs can be asked to do demonstration lessons, and the hiring manager can see the person *doing their job*—not a hypothetical, but the actual job. In a teaching demonstration lesson, the teaching candidate does not know the students, which can inject some degree of challenge, but the debrief after the lesson is still rooted in actual teacher choices and not a simulation. Chapter 8 lays out a detailed method of selecting teachers who have high potential to be excellent teachers. However, there is no analog for leadership candidates that is based in something experiential. The leadership candidate can't run a real meeting of teachers. There can be hypothetical scenarios posed, and yes, candidates can distinguish themselves somewhat based on how deeply they analyze content and pedagogy. But these are only two elements of expertise of an instructional leader. The other two—being expert in youth development and adult development—are much harder to discern.

As described earlier, content and pedagogy are prerequisites for instructional leadership. But how to push adults to improve—the work of leading—is won or lost with how good the leader is at understanding adult development. You don't even get to the table unless you are expert in what to teach and how to teach. *To know a leader—to know a leader's potential—is to know him or her in the dimensions of youth and adult development.*

So how can you determine people's skill at adult development? Can you do this in an interview? An interview and a follow-up? What set of experiences would suffice? While there is no certain number of conversations, the answer is clear: you need to see them try over time to change long-term patterns of adult behavior. To know them really well is to know how they react during authentic times of stress. This is when beliefs get tested and leaders start to look either externally or internally. And this is precisely why the Artisan Teaching system described in this book is such a good fit for identifying emerging leaders.

## Simultaneously Learning to Teach and Learning to Lead

By pushing almost all efforts thorough this small collaborative team, each teacher gets known very well by someone (the Team Leader) who, by virtue of his or her own experience, *is built to look for the right indicators.* One of the most telling statistics at AMS is not the number of internal leadership hires (all leadership promotions and hires have been internal) but that there were no regrets in those hires precisely because there was no guesswork. We test drove each of them for four or five years.

The key to school and system sustainability is the internal development of leaders. So far in this book, we have described the system, including the expertise needed to lead, the structures needed to collaborate, and the time needed to accomplish this. We also have looked at the results and have linked the key result of sustainability to the consistent production of Team Leaders. What it comes down to, however, is for the *right* people to emerge. Certain people are the game changers here, and it behooves school leaders not just to set up the system but to be fully attentive to all signs of emerging leadership qualities. The school needs to notice the right people, grab on, and lead them inexorably to the role of Team Leader. This is the crowning piece of the entire system. The vehicle (the Artisan Teaching collaborative teams) is there for teachers to emerge. The right people (Team Leaders) lead these meetings. The qualifications to become a Team Leader are clearly known and publicized. To tie the whole thing together, the Team Leader, while leading the team, needs to keep leadership constantly in mind and must notice, and deliberately encourage, those with the right stuff—and this is where it gets really hard.

## Trajectory of Developing the Next Generation of Team Leaders

The environment of teaching is complex and emotional, and this mix doesn't always bring out the best in everybody. Therefore, determining the next TL—especially early on—is not a slam dunk by any means. Although several fine studies of leadership are available, the emerging leadership mindset does not lend itself to a checklist approach. Checking for qualities is after-the-fact stuff, once the mindset has already been established. During the Artisan Teaching apprenticeship process, each teacher is being trained in a leadership mindset from the beginning. But the process is delicate and entirely differentiated, and therefore the organization needs to be good at identifying highly contextualized indicators. That is the job we describe next. The job is inherently difficult because the school is *looking for real indicators of school leadership, perhaps well before the teacher has attained even proficiency as a teacher.* So what indicators do TLs look for and at what pace? What does this look and sound like when it works? We answer these questions next.

The Team Leader bears the biggest responsibility in determining who the next series of TLs will be. As such, the Team Leader has the following three jobs:

- *Assess* early on the leadership potential of each teacher on the team.
- *Encourage* the highest-potential teachers through an early and sustained conversation on school leadership.
- *Engage* the highest-potential teachers in specific school-based leadership activities that develop their leadership competencies.

## Job 1: Assess teachers early on so that no high-potential teacher will go unnoticed.

Let's consider a detailed chronology of assessing a teacher for high potential, from 0 to 12 months. Note, however, that this timeline is flexible and allows teachers and schools to develop artisanship at different paces. This assessment of a high-potential teacher could occur during the teacher's first year of teaching or later on in the teacher's career, if potential emerges more gradually; or when the teacher is hired at a new school; or when a school begins to implement the Artisan Teaching model. In any event, the team system and TL-teacher relationship provides the structure to discover almost all observable leadership potential.

### 0–6 months: First tiny drops from leadership pipeline

Let's call our teacher "Hi-Po," for "High-Potential" teacher. It's two weeks into the school year and the honeymoon is over, with student misbehaviors mounting daily. Hi-Po started the year inconsistently stating behavioral expectations, and now students are really starting to push back. With each day, students sense that Hi-Po has a little less authority, and Hi-Po is growing frustrated. Her class is calling out, getting up, and talking across the room. Flying paper balls are next. The TL is *daily* going into Hi-Po's classroom and providing consistent suggestions, and Hi-Po takes the advice at the start of each lesson and clearly states a few key expectations, and then attempts to hold students accountable. Almost unimportant is whether the student behavior improves immediately.

Even in this scenario, indicators can be seen. Here's where teacher development and leadership identification perhaps first intertwine: even if the advice does not translate into immediate improvement and Hi-Po continues to struggle, the question becomes, is Hi-Po undergoing good struggle or bad struggle? "Bad struggle" would be evidenced, for example, by the teacher not implementing the recommendations, then getting frustrated and creating additional problems, perhaps by trying a different strategy. "Good struggle" would be trying the recommendations—in this case, giving clear expectations and then following up, sometimes in the moment, sometimes after class with consequences. The struggle here is to have the patience to see a strategy through. Teachers with high potential will exhibit this good struggle.

By the six-month mark, student behaviors should be improved, and—this is crucial—Hi-Po can *appreciate the struggle* to establish consistency. This evolution is about more than simply getting students to behave better. And this is not about Hi-Po complying with her boss. This is *a nascent awareness by Hi-Po that she has a grasp on her own learning.* At this point, Hi-Po starts to see that it is not about the students and their behavior, but about how smart and consistent routines can affect student outcomes. It is Hi-Po's genuine belief, tested with real classrooms in real time over many months (as opposed to during an interview), that her actions determine students' actions. She may not yet be able to get the behavior (or learning) that she fully wants, but she knows that she has the power—and obligation—to do so. A teacher cannot "yes" her way through these six months. The highest of high-potentials realize and accept that they are learning to learn.

Also during the first six months, the TL is heavily pushing the value of student thinking. The TL is essentially marinating the entire team in a rich conversation that elevates the importance of getting students to think. Almost every conversation includes discussion of students bearing the cognitive load. It's crucial to not wait until classroom management is good to talk about this—it must be done concurrently.

During the first six months, the TL is also meeting regularly with an assistant principal. In a sort of "nested model," the TL is simultaneously working in an apprenticeship with a principal or assistant principal, receiving the same collaborative support that teachers receive from TLs. The discussions and mentorship in these meetings are about progress of all teachers, and there is a standing agenda item on identification of hi-pos. The principal, in turn, holds regular meetings with the assistant principals whose entire agenda is dedicated to hi-po's.

## 6–12 months: Bigger drops from the pipeline

During months 6–12, it starts to become clear if the teacher is internalizing the need to put the cognitive load on students. At weekly planning meetings, Hi-Po starts to offer ideas that foster student thinking, and she may politely and smartly "push back" on an inadequate lesson plan presented by a team member. Even if Hi-Po nuanced this criticism and couched it with incredible delicacy, this suggestion needs to be the shot heard around the school: "Hi-Po said *what* at a team meeting?" The TL will hear Hi-Po's objection as if someone banged a giant gong, and TL in turn will sound it to the assistant principal, who then relays it to the principal. Principal: "She said *what* to *whom*? Nice!" The antennae and apparatus now orient a little more toward Hi-Po. Senior leadership wants to know more.

Hi-Po starts to produce higher-quality work and thought that reflects team conclusions. Hi-Po offers a great idea for an end-of-unit project, and, without being told that it might help, Hi-Po played soccer after school with her most difficult student, and accounts of both events make it back to the principal's ear.

Hi-Po will come to meetings excited to share reports of students making connections and challenging their own misconceptions. She is excited when students take charge of their learning and shares this excitement with her peers. The TL will notice this enthusiasm and deliberately highlight this developmental adult thinking. TL will nimbly shift the conversation toward the best idea. TL will deliberately model for Hi-Po how to talk to a teacher who is not catching on to the school's vision of high-quality instruction.

Although these meetings are in name and in actuality collaborative, this quality does not mean that each person and each idea gets equal air time. From an organizational quality perspective, some ideas are better than others. Specifically, the more consistent the idea is with the school's vision of teaching and learning, the better the idea; and ideas that externalize locus of control are not tolerated. Hi-Po will notice that the TL is stressing internal locus of control and higher-order thinking and will start to use the language of both.

Hi-Po will find the TL during times outside the regularly scheduled meetings to ask genuine questions about both concepts, not to object but to understand further—another huge gong that needs to reverberate up to the principal. This conversation will then naturally expand to include team dynamics and even more refined analysis of lessons. The TL will foreshadow curricular conversations with Hi-Po, almost developing a subtext to the main conversation. Hi-Po is starting to get pulled along toward leadership.

## Job 2: Encourage the highest-potential teachers through an early, sustained, and appropriate conversation on school leadership.

As adult learners in the Artisan Teaching model, high-potential teachers are focusing on the craft of teaching. The TL, who is simultaneously developing teaching and leadership qualities, must give appropriate shape to a conversation about school leadership.

The key to this conversation is to be extremely careful in what gets praise. A lack of student achievement data at first is expected. Not unlike coaching a baseball player, the refinement of fundamentals (e.g., a level swing, driving the ball with the body momentum as opposed to wrist muscle) is prerequisite to achieving sustained excellent batting average. Similarly, the TL needs to be listening for teacher choices that reveal great fundamentals—an internal locus of control, teacher choices that do not pass the blame to students—and the TL needs to praise these choices at team meetings in great detail and with great fanfare. If the focus of praise is on immediate data, then high-potential teachers will seek more praise and in doing so will try to get great data as opposed to developing the habits that will generate useful data. At first, praise the adult behavior we want to see, not the student results we want to see.

## Job 3: Engage high-potential teachers in specific school-based leadership activities that develop their leadership competencies.

Roughly around the end of year 2, Hi-Po is starting to distance herself from the group. Student data are surging, great fundamentals are in place, and the teacher has been receiving praise for improving and for having a strong internal locus of control. Now it's time to give this teacher a taste of leading adults. This responsibility should be small but include, even in trace amounts, the key quality of true school leadership: the challenge of changing long-term habits of adult behavior.

The inclusion of this goal—even at a modest level—is what distinguishes school leadership from mere school coordination. Undoubtedly, this assignment will involve frustration. Anyone who has ever led in the school context can vouch for the fact that changing long-term patterns of adult behavior is exceedingly difficult. Therefore, the choice of leadership activity needs to be made carefully. It needs to surface just the right amount of adult resistance—enough so that the resistance is clear, but not so much that the resistance seems insurmountable.

A good first challenge in leadership could be to coach a fourth-year teacher, traditional in approach, who prefers teacher-centered lessons. This teacher could also have something of an independent streak. The leadership challenge could be to help this teacher design and lead one student-centered project. Although Hi-Po would be working with just one teacher on just one specific project, it would allow her to feel the dynamic of adult change, and it would also allow the TL to have a well-defined adult learning activity. TL and Hi-Po could work on this project together for a month, mining the activity for as much leadership learning as possible.

## Iteration and Scaling Up

In this chapter, we have discussed the identification and support of one high-potential teacher in her progression through the Artisan Teaching system into the role of Team Leader. This process, as we explained, is the heart of the system. But the driving force of the Artisan Teaching model is in its ability to repeat this process over time, continually multiplying the number of instructional leaders in the school, all sharing precisely the same beliefs and instructional vision. Although the system envisions a years-long process of leadership development, requiring a leader to provide intensive support for only a small number of teachers, the impact on a schoolwide level can be huge because the system results in a perpetual *doubling* of the number of Team Leaders over the course of several years.

Indeed, it is this iterative nature of the Artisan Teaching system that reveals its full power and how the school can thrive by continually developing new leaders. We have found that even when a leader works with three teachers this intently, two of the teachers usually will not get to be TLs. One might become a proficient teacher but may not want to engage in adult leadership. Another may leave the school due to normal workplace realities (e.g., moving out of state or choosing to return to graduate school). But typically, we develop one newly minted Team Leader from this group of three within about three years. We argue that in an iterative system, one new Team Leader is all you need. To start this work, the school needs at a minimum one leader who possesses expertise in content, pedagogy, youth development, and adult development and who has a vision of instructional excellence that is so clear and so deeply internalized that the leader can spot the highest-quality instruction almost instinctually. The leader needs to commit to a several-year process to lead two collaborative teams and, as a result, develop at least two new superb Team Leaders after three years.

To be sure, all teachers benefit from being on the team, but often one on each team will emerge to become a TL. It is important to note that this is a choice: instead of the leader trying to make a large portion of the teaching staff a little bit better every year, the choice for this leader is to work with these two small teams of a few high-potentials.

Now to iterate this process for our leadership pipeline: with no loss of fidelity to vision, these two new TLs then carry on the process with two teams each themselves, and so on. Going back, if we start this exponential sequence with two superb instructional leaders, then after six years you have 2 (the original TLs) + 4 (the new TLs). After six years, you have 2 (original who now exclusively mentor TLs) + 4 (second-generation TLs) + 8 (third-generation TLs), for 14 superb instructional leaders. Even assuming some natural attrition, as some people begin families or move to new cities, the number of instructional leaders within the school continues to grow exponentially, creating a critical mass of core excellence that will drive a school forward, we argue, in perpetuity.

## The Results of the Artisan Teaching Model: Leaders Are Made, Not Hired

We believe that developing teachers and leaders is, in a way, the same work—two sides of one coin. The prevailing wisdom is a bit different. Many educators discuss these as problems with two different solutions. "Teacher development" is commonly understood to have a variety of components: new teacher mentoring, professional development, data analysis, classroom management support, and observation/feedback cycles. "Leadership training" is often discussed as a separate phenomenon. Schools are constantly "looking for" new leaders from other schools, or considering which of their most effective teachers would be best for a move into a leadership role, where they will begin training adults in leadership for the very first time. And this new role, for most teachers, is a significant change.

We suggest a new paradigm. All of the work of developing teachers is more effective when the various components are blended into one collaborative system that matches the way adults learn most effectively. Moreover, all of the difficult and rigorous work that we describe in this book, where teachers are pushed to work together to solve the problems they face and discuss daily issues with colleagues, is the *work of leadership*. Not every teacher can be an effective instructional leader, but a school needs to try to make a leader out of every teacher with such potential. And by viewing the work this way, a school can leverage an apprenticeship system (which engages all of its teachers in this work simultaneously) to create a new pipeline of emerging leaders at the same time as it is developing its new cadre of great teachers.

Indeed, all mentoring conversations have two participants. At any given moment, each participant is thinking about his or her own teaching in the classroom, listening to another teacher's thoughts on instruction, and thereby improving *as a teacher*. Simultaneously, each participant is also thinking about how to collaborate effectively, how to share an opinion in a manner that will positively influence the other adult, and how to demonstrate effective practice; each is thereby improving *as a leader*. When we dramatically increase the frequency and importance of these conversations within a school building, we are also dramatically increasing the development of both teachers and leaders.

We contend that the most common school structures effectively block leadership pipelines. Consider the typical school leadership structure, with a top-down view of the roles of administrators and teachers. A typical small school with, say, 50 teachers and 4 instructional leaders, has teachers work mostly in isolation (aside from professional development meetings and some collegial mentoring), but they receive ample support and thoughtful feedback from the four school administrators. There are well-functioning (but not collaborative) schools with an approximately 12:1 teacher-to-leader ratio that consistently post fine results without the collaborative structure that we describe.

But consider the longer-term impact of this typical school structure. Suppose that the teachers in this school work for three, four, or five years with this view of instructional feedback and support coming almost exclusively from school administrators. After a few years of this work, this typical school will often need to find a new principal or assistant principal for some reason or another. And at that moment, the school leaders will look at their teachers and try to predict which teacher *might* make an effective leader. Even in a well-functioning school with good achievement results, this group of teachers has devoted several years of hard work learning to teach students, but they have not developed the skills necessary for teaching adults—that is, the core skills of leadership. If this school hopes to find a new leader, they will need to begin training one of their best teachers for a completely new role, or they will seek to hire a new leader from outside the school who developed leadership skills elsewhere. This is the problem that so many schools face—and this dilemma can lead to a gradual (or sudden) decline of a successful school.

But consider the results of the Artisan Teaching system. The teachers begin working in collaborative teams from their very first day of teaching. Even during the first few years of their careers (when the primary focus is on learning effective classroom practices), the teachers are forced to develop collaboration skills. They learn to reflect on feedback every day; they learn how to push back when a teammate shares an idea that isn't good enough; they learn how to speak with a frustrated teammate; they learn how to let the best idea win. In any given conversation, they might serve as the mentor or the mentee.

Over time, that dynamic gradually shifts, with the most successful teachers tilting more often toward mentor. Over the years, this person's voice in collaborative meetings is gradually viewed with more authority and weight—not because of positional authority, but because of *earned* authority. The quality of the teacher's instruction and results are evident, and the teacher is becoming skilled at sharing ideas with colleagues in team meetings. With that authority, a more experienced teacher will gradually learn how to share ideas with less-experienced teachers, and will spend several years learning what types of support those developing teachers need. Even without a formal mentoring role, this is the expectation of every teacher at the school, because that is how teams function. Over the course of these years of teaching in the Artisan Teaching system, a veteran teacher might work with three, four, or five teammates, each with different skills and learning styles. This work of collaboration simultaneously develops leadership alongside teaching. It is one process.

We previously have discussed the impact of the Artisan Teaching system on teachers' instruction and students' achievement: teaching is respected as a craft; new teachers are mentored; students achieve at high rates; curriculum is shared and improved in a consistent manner; professional development, mentoring, and discipline support are merged into a single, comprehensive system of support; and a collegial tone permeates the school.

But the most important benefit of this system addresses one of the most glaring problems for school improvement: the sustainability of a school's success through the development of new leaders. Using the Artisan Teaching model, the most successful teachers are the most successful collaborators. The most successful teachers develop leadership skills every day of their teaching careers. After three to five years of successful teaching and collaboration, when the administrators have no doubt that a teacher effectively represents the instructional vision of the school, they will assign that teacher the role of Team Leader—although the teacher has, at that point, already been leading conversations and mentoring other teachers effectively for several years. And after several more years of work as an effective Team Leader, along with a similar system of collaborative support for the entire group of Team Leaders, the school's most effective teachers and the school's most effective leaders develop in parallel. They are the same people engaged in the same process that yields both results.

When an Artisan Teaching school needs to identify a new assistant principal, the school identifies the Team Leader who is interested (and licensed) to continue the same development that began 5 to 10 years earlier. The new administrator earns a new title, but very little needs to change in the role itself. Of course, they might need to attend a training session in order to supervise a noninstructional task such as budgeting, purchasing, or compliance work that needs to be completed. But the core role of school leaders is instruction, and these Team Leaders already reflect the instructional mission of the school, possess an incredibly strong growth mindset, and enjoy the great respect of the entire school community—before ever interviewing for a school leadership position. They have already apprenticed in leading the school's instructional development for several years. Their role as a Team Leader continues uninterrupted—and the school has no need to consider external candidates for leadership positions.

In the end, it turns out that a system designed to support teacher development in the most effective manner will also serve to develop new, like-minded instructional leaders. This system serves many purposes for students and teachers alike—but most important, it creates a real system of leadership training, with a coherent vision of instruction spreading throughout the school, and a leadership pipeline that creates a truly sustainable school.

## Chapter 5

**Question:** *This book describes the process of identifying new Team Leaders. But I don't understand where the training happens. How are new Team Leaders trained for the new role? How does this work lead to the training of people who are qualified to become assistant principals and principals?*

**Answer:** One of the most fundamental principles underlying the Artisan Teaching approach is that people learn most effectively when they do engaging, relevant work in collaboration with experts. This is true of students who work on authentic and engaging tasks with a great teacher's support—which is more effective than isolated and inauthentic lessons. It is true of teachers who work together on collaborative teams with highly successful teachers—which is more effective than sending teachers to large-group professional development sessions that are separate from their real, day-to-day experiences. And, it is equally true for aspiring leaders.

The Artisan Teaching approach develops its new leaders by immersing them in a years-long process of collaboration—not by removing them from their daily work for separate training. All new Team Leaders in the apprenticeship structure have spent two to three years on collaborative teams, observing the Team Leader's mentoring and feedback, planning lessons together with a team, and learning about adult development in real time. We believe that the Artisan Teaching model is designed for development at all levels, because all adults are working within the same system simultaneously, and all changes of roles and titles all occur within the same structure that envelops all of their work.

# PART II

Customizing and Implementing
the Artisan Teaching Model

# 6

# Customizing the Model to Fit Any School

Given that schools are generally operating at capacity, with teachers and administrators fully assigned, deployed, and often exhausted, no new effort—especially the approach presented in this book—can be rolled out *in addition* to everything else school leaders do. Where implemented, it needs to be used *instead of* other, less-effective leadership practices.

Moreover, with typical school budgets tightly constrained or shrinking, it is crucial for school reform efforts to be revenue neutral. With this point in mind, it is crucial to note that AMS has utilized the Artisan Teaching model with no additional funding or resources beyond the typical school budget. AMS is located in one of the lowest-income communities in the United States, with little ability to supplement the operating budget. Also, as will become clear in this chapter, AMS has a "tall" school structure (serving seven grade levels, but with fewer than 100 students in each grade), making it the most challenging scenario for implementation. Yet the model has thrived at AMS. In other words, if it can be done at AMS, it can be done anywhere.

In this chapter, we provide several strategies on what to reduce, eliminate, and shave so that any school can customize an implementation of the Artisan Teaching model that makes sense for its specific situation and challenges. We also present ideal staffing ratios and key techniques for any size school, and provide specific, detailed strategies for the unique challenges of small-school implementation.

## How to Allocate Time for Team Leadership

The Artisan Teaching model does not require additional staffing—only shifts in the roles and assignments of the staff that a school's budget allows. The principle underlying the scheduling of the Artisan Teaching model is to reorganize the time of the Team Leaders, allowing them to devote a major portion of their time to work with only one or two instructional teams. Instructional leaders in the Artisan Teaching model cannot provide instructional support for an entire school or conduct meaningful mentoring or professional development for 10, 20, or 30 teachers on a staff. Indeed, we believe that such support is superficial and fundamentally different from real, in-depth collaboration. The apprenticeship model that we describe requires us to make available one Team Leader who will provide all of the various supports that a few teachers normally might receive from a wide range of leaders. Simply put, the model requires us to reorganize the assignments of adults who traditionally provide small amounts of support to a large number of teachers so that, instead, each can provide a large amount of support to only a small number of teachers.

Figures 6.1 and 6.2 roughly illustrate the typical time allocation for a content coach working within the typical school model and within the Artisan Teaching model, respectively. These pie charts can serve as a guide for reassigning the work of leaders within the school.

You may tap a variety of methods to create the extra time in the schedules of instructional leaders to complete the work of Team Leader—at least one hour per day for each team that they lead. Schools can utilize a mix of these strategies, depending on their staff's strengths and areas of expertise. Indeed, AMS has used virtually all of the strategies we describe in this chapter at different times, always adjusting its plans to fit the needs and capacity of the staff in any given year.

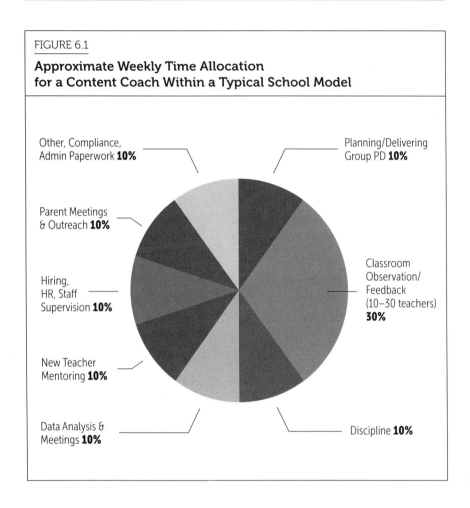

FIGURE 6.1

**Approximate Weekly Time Allocation
for a Content Coach Within a Typical School Model**

Other, Compliance, Admin Paperwork **10%**

Planning/Delivering Group PD **10%**

Parent Meetings & Outreach **10%**

Classroom Observation/ Feedback (10–30 teachers) **30%**

Hiring, HR, Staff Supervision **10%**

New Teacher Mentoring **10%**

Data Analysis & Meetings **10%**

Discipline **10%**

# Strategies to Employ the Artisan Teaching Model

In the following pages, we provide a series of examples of programming shifts (before Artisan Teaching and with Artisan Teaching) to demonstrate that the model is feasible using the same overall number of staff that a typical school employs. The left column describes approximate breakdowns of the time each employee typically might spend on a variety of roles, in order to demonstrate how that time could be repurposed to implement the new model.

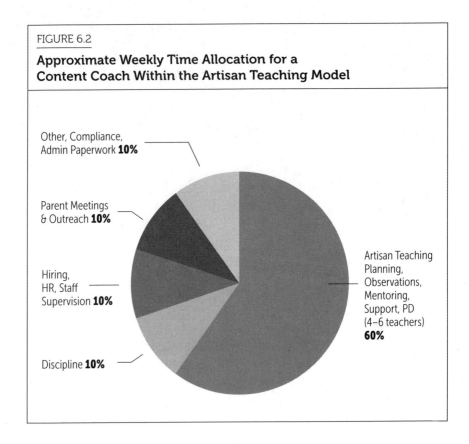

FIGURE 6.2

**Approximate Weekly Time Allocation for a Content Coach Within the Artisan Teaching Model**

Other, Compliance, Admin Paperwork **10%**

Parent Meetings & Outreach **10%**

Hiring, HR, Staff Supervision **10%**

Discipline **10%**

Artisan Teaching Planning, Observations, Mentoring, Support, PD (4–6 teachers) **60%**

## Strategy 1: Adjust the roles of full-time administrators to serve as Team Leaders.

This is the simplest and most straightforward strategy. Most schools have at least one administrator who could serve as a Team Leader for one or two teams with only a small change in time allocation. This strategy is particularly logical for a hypothetical middle school that has a "6th grade assistant principal" and a "7th grade assistant principal," or a high school that has an "assistant principal for English" and an "assistant principal for math." These administrators likely already spend much of their time supporting teachers in their area of administration, mentoring new teachers, assisting with discipline for those teachers, and planning

PD and data meetings for their grades or departments. These other roles can be reduced, allowing them to shift their responsibilities—thereby spending most of their time working as Team Leader for two teams that match their area of expertise. Most schools could easily identify one or two administrators, who could shift their roles to focus on one or two teams, instead of the traditional grade-wide or subject-area administrative role.

| Typical Role and Time Allocation | Artisan Teaching Role and Time Allocation |
| --- | --- |
| **Assistant Principal 1** (with grade-wide responsibility for 7th grade) | **Assistant Principal 1** (working as TL for two teams in area of expertise) |
| • 25% observations and classroom support for all teachers in the 7th grade | • 40% TL for 7th and 8th grade math teams (including observations, mentoring, and support only for those four teachers) <br> • 20% other schoolwide instructional support (as needed) |
| • 25% discipline and emergencies | • 25% discipline and emergencies |
| • 25% planning weekly, schoolwide PD sessions for all math teachers | • 0% planning weekly, schoolwide PD sessions for all math teachers (PD is incorporated into team meetings) |
| • 25% administrative work, compliance paperwork, HR, data analysis, and weekly data meetings with staff | • 15% administrative work, compliance paperwork, HR (the data meetings are canceled and incorporated into team meetings) |

| Assistant Principal 2 (with grade-wide responsibility for 8th grade) | Assistant Principal 2 (working as TL for two teams in area of expertise) |
|---|---|
| • 25% observations and class-room support for all teachers in the 8th grade | • 40% TL for 7th and 8th grade English teams (including observations, mentoring, and support for those four teachers in both grades)<br>• 20% other schoolwide instruc-tional support |
| • 25% discipline and emergencies | • 25% discipline and emergencies |
| • 25% planning weekly, school-wide PD sessions for all math teachers | • 0% planning weekly, school-wide PD sessions for all math teachers (PD is incorporated into team meetings) |
| • 25% administrative work, compliance paperwork, HR, data analysis, and weekly data meetings with staff | • 15% administrative work, compliance paperwork, HR (the data meetings are can-celed and incorporated into team meetings) |
| **Summary of Traditional Structure**<br>No collaborative planning teams exist. Teachers have grade-wide and subject-area meetings every week, and occasional observa-tions from an assistant principal. | **Summary with Artisan Teaching Model**<br>This strategy provides Artisan Teaching Team Leaders for the 7th grade math teachers, the 8th grade math teachers, the 7th grade English teachers, and the 8th grade English teachers. Four teams are led by the school's two assistant principals, without requiring any staffing changes. |

> With only this one shift in roles of the two assistant principals, we have created teams for approximately half of the teachers in the 7th and 8th grades (all of the math and English teachers, as well as any special education teachers working with those teams). All of these teachers now receive support from an assistant principal who is only responsible for supporting those two teams' teachers on a daily basis.

## Strategy 2: Shift an instructional coach to teach one class and lead the team.

Another straightforward strategy that allows a school to shift an existing staff member's responsibilities to lead a collaborative team is to consider a full-time "staff developer," "coach," or other out-of-classroom role—people who are excellent teachers with ample experience and already provide many of the supports and leadership roles described in this book. By reassigning 25 percent of this coach's time to teaching one section of a course, the school accomplishes various objectives. First, the coach joins the apprenticeship team for the class he or she is teaching. Second, this approach reduces the teaching assignment of one of the other teachers, thereby allowing that teacher to play a new role (which can be one of the roles previously completed by the coach). Finally, this strategy is a great way to create an apprenticeship team when only one teacher previously taught the course. In other words, if a school has only one 9th grade English teacher (teaching all five sections of the 9th grade English course), it is impossible to implement the Artisan Teaching model. The coach taking one course of 9th grade English solves the problem.

This table provides an example of this strategy:

Consider a school that employs a full-time staff developer (a "coach") to provide professional development, training, and mentoring for one subject-area department across all grade levels. A logical strategy for implementation of the Artisan Teaching model is to recognize that the coach's support is more effective when working as a collaborative TL with only one or two grades. The teachers in the other grades will get less support from the coach, because they will have their own TL. This plan could work with a coach, a staff developer, a reading specialist, or an assistant principal, depending on the staffing needs and capabilities of the school.

| Typical Role and Time Allocation | Artisan Teaching Role and Time Allocation |
|---|---|
| **High School English Coach** (assigned to provide support to the entire school's English teachers) | **High School English Coach** (now teaching one period of 9th grade English, and allocating most time exclusively to the 9th grade English team) |
| • 40% instructional and classroom support for English teachers (spread equally among all of the English teachers in grades 9, 10, 11, and 12) | • 60% teaching one class per day of 9th grade English, and serving as TL for the team<br>• 20% small amount of additional support for the 10th, 11th, and 12th grade English teams (mostly consulting with other TLs) |
| • 30% planning and delivering weekly PD sessions for all English teachers in all grades | • 0% weekly PD meetings—these are canceled and incorporated into the apprenticeship model. PD for the 9th grade teachers is included in the time above. |

| | |
|---|---|
| • 30% miscellaneous administrative work, including coordinating administration of periodic reading assessments or some other roles | • 20% miscellaneous administrative work; this work is reduced by reassigning the organization of the periodic reading assessments to the other 9th grade English teacher (who has a reduced teaching assignment as a result of the coach teaching one of her classes). |
| **9th Grade English Teaching staff** (one teacher) | **9th Grade English Teaching Staff** (one teacher and the coach) |
| • Teaches five periods of 9th grade English | • Teacher teaches four periods of 9th grade English, with one extra period off per day<br>• Instead of one period of teaching, the teacher is assigned a new role of coordinating the administration of the school-wide periodic reading assessments (taking over that role from the English coach) |
| • Attends weekly PD session for all English teachers | • Weekly PD session for English teachers is canceled. Time is used for an apprenticeship meeting. |
| **Summary of Traditional Structure** <br> One teacher is responsible for all five sections of 9th grade English, with no teammate and | **Summary Using Artisan Teaching Model** <br> Instead of spending small amounts of time with a large number of teachers, the English |

| Summary of Traditional Structure (*cont.*) | Summary Using Artisan Teaching Model (*cont.*) |
| --- | --- |
| no opportunity for collaboration. The teacher receives a small amount of support from an English coach, who is responsible for working with all teachers across the entire school. | coach now focuses more than half of the workday on supporting *only* the 9th grade English team. The TL teaches one section of the course, gets to know the curriculum and students, and meets every day with the other teacher/teammate. They share a classroom and review every lesson plan in advance. Because the teacher has a reduced teaching load, he or she takes on one of the coach's leadership roles. Weekly PD meetings are no longer necessary. |

Although a coach or assistant principal might be able to teach one or two classes each, schools will need additional leadership capacity to provide TLs for a full-scale or even half-scale implementation of Artisan Teaching. These TLs need to come from the current full-time teaching corps and must be given the time needed to lead a team—time needed to hold meetings, to visit classrooms, to hold debrief conversations, and so forth. Therefore, the TL/teachers must have reduced teaching assignments. Depending on the circumstances, it could be that the teacher teaches one or two fewer classes a day, which means that every two or three team leaders who are "made" from the corps of teachers will require an additional teacher to pick up untaught classes. The funds to hire an extra teacher might be available simply by shifting the school's budgeting priorities. At AMS, the time for teacher collaboration is the *first* budget priority, and, therefore, some money is shifted from other expenses.

## Strategy 3: Eliminate reduced-time teacher roles that are unnecessary within the Artisan Teaching model.

Another strategy can account for the necessary reduced teaching load: determining and then eliminating existing reduced-time teacher roles that become redundant within the Artisan Teaching model. Two such roles are that of "grade team leader" and "content-area leader." It is common practice in schools to organize vertically (by department) and horizontally (by grade). We believe that although the four subject-area teachers of a particular grade could have a common agenda (e.g., discussing challenging students that they teach in common, or designing cross-curricular projects), this is not what teachers want to, or should be, talking about. We believe that it is far more important for a teacher's development to meet for long periods of time with people *who do the exact same job.*

In order for a 6th grade math teacher, say, to become a true artisan, he or she needs to talk about, reflect upon, and devote huge effort into improving the planning and delivery of 6th grade math lessons. As well intentioned as colleagues can be, meeting with the 6th grade English teacher or the 8th grade math teacher will not address the overwhelming and dominant adult needs of a 6th grade math teacher. The 6th grade math teacher's opportunities to get much better, we believe, do not lie in vertical alignment discussions or cross-grade planning. The teacher will learn to be an artisan through highly focused, extensive conversation and introspection that addresses *his or her performance* daily. These practices can be found in the apprenticeship team. In the Artisan Teaching model, we do not have "grade team leaders" or "department heads." Instead, the teachers who would otherwise be grade team leaders and department heads now become Team Leaders in the new model. When true cross-collaboration is needed or desired, then the TLs will have that conversation among themselves, thereby critically allowing teachers to maintain laserlike focus on one thing: how they can make the next day's lesson as good as it can be.

The following table summarizes this third strategy:

In this scenario, a school uses the Artisan Teaching model to eliminate grade-level meetings and traditional departmental meetings, repurposing this time to lead team meetings.

| Typical Role and Time Allocation | Artisan Teaching Role and Time Allocation |
|---|---|
| **Grade-level Leader—6th Grade** | **6th Grade Math Team Leader in Artisan Teaching Model** |
| • 80% teaching 6th grade (any subject) | • 80% teaching 6th grade math |
| • 20% planning for and leading grade-level meeting for 6th grade teachers. At these meetings, all 6th grade teachers (all subjects) are present. | • 20% planning for and leading teams. Meetings are attended only by those teachers who teach the exact same subject and grade. Maximum size = four (including TL). |
| • One teacher receives a reduced teaching load (typically one class per day) to plan for and then hold meetings twice a week with a group of 6th grade teachers across subjects on one grade. Agenda items may include looking at student work across disciplines, discussing logistics of field trips, discussing at-risk students as a 6th grade team, or discussing schoolwide PD initiatives (e.g., "increase accountable talk") as it relates to 6th grade. | • Grade level approaches to schoolwide PD initiatives such as "increasing accountable talk" or discussion of field trip logistics are eliminated; all work is differentiated, highly targeted PD for each team and each teacher based on specific adult learning needs and specific teacher deficits. |

| Typical Role and Time Allocation | Artisan Teaching Role and Time Allocation |
|---|---|
| Math Department Head for Grades 9–12 | 9th Grade TL in Artisan Teaching Model |
| • One teacher receives a reduced teaching load (typically one or two classes per day) to plan for and hold "department meetings." Agenda items may include vertically aligning the curriculum, general sharing of math teaching best practices (no particular grade), and training on use of graphing calculators or other technology applicable to multiple grades. | • Eliminated from agenda are vertical alignment of curriculum (TLs do this on their own) and knowledge-based training such as how to use technology. Instead, all work is differentiated, highly targeted PD for each team and each teacher based on specific adult learning needs and specific teacher deficits. |

## Ratios of Teachers to Team Leaders

When actually forming teams, the fundamental question arises, "Given the nature of the team's work, how many team members is ideal?" Because of the necessary intensity of the relationship between the TL and group members, the TL will need to spend many hours working informally with each of her team members, in addition to the formally scheduled team meetings. These are times for the TL to engage in the highest-impact adult development activities—modeling lessons, observing the teacher, role-playing, giving feedback, analyzing student work, and engaging in rehearsal cycles. These are each time-intensive activities, and the TL will aggregate all of his or her nonteaching time to doing these high-impact activities with teachers. Each teacher needs roughly seven hours of TL support a week. To do so, the TL will use five periods off per week (reduced teacher time) plus her five prep periods and four additional hours usually devoted to whole-school PD, departmental meetings, and grade-level meetings. With our schedule, that translates to approximately 17 hours of time available to work with *three teachers*. Each teacher attends the group team meeting (two hours total), and each teacher then gets an additional five hours of one-on-one time with the TL. This makes a total of 17 hours. *The maximum ratio of teachers to TLs in this system is 3:1.* If the TL gets a further reduction of teaching load, then the TL could lead an additional team as well.

With this basic ratio, we can now examine how this might play out given various school sizes. To start, let's consider a secondary school, organized by subject, with roughly 300 students per grade. The type of scheduling (block or classic) and number of grades in the school are not important factors in this example. Further suppose that for each grade there are 25 students per class and three teachers for the grade who each teach four sections. This means that the school would need one TL for each subject in this grade. In a sense, this scenario fits the model like a glove.

Next, let's consider a larger school, one with 600 or even 900 students on a grade. It follows that the model just described for 300 students in a grade can be extended simply by multiplying as needed. That is, with 900 students in a grade, three TLs would be needed to cover the situation with the same ratio. Suppose the scenario is 450 students in a grade in a middle school serving grades 7 and 8. In this case, there would be one TL for grade 7, one for grade 8, and another TL who would split a small 7th grade team and a small 8th grade team.

## Implications for Small Schools

The toughest scenario in which to implement the Artisan Teaching model is with truly small schools, or schools with small numbers of students on each grade. Many schools—including a large number of elementary schools, charter schools, and virtually all of the schools in the "new small schools movement" in New York City—serve approximately

80 to 110 students in each grade level. There are also many larger schools that divide their building into smaller "academies," thereby creating several small communities of a similar size. In all of these cases, the small size—approximately 100 students—is carefully designed to provide an effective learning community. Indeed, research demonstrates that a school with approximately 100 students at each grade/age level creates a community where the students and adults all know one another and effective learning can occur.

Although the small school model can provide significant benefits for the development of community among the students, we suggest that it has inadvertently and unintentionally increased professional isolation in the work that matters most—the planning of lessons and the engagement in the highest-impact discussions and activities that improve teacher practice. Virtually all of the small secondary schools in New York City (both public and charter) employ a model of *one teacher* teaching all sections of each academic course at each grade level. That is, schools with approximately 100 students in each grade generally have three, four, or five class sections in those grades. Over the course of the day, there are, say, four sections of 9th grade English, four sections of 9th grade history, four sections of 9th grade math, and four sections of 9th grade science. In all of these schools, the ubiquitous model (and the simplest model) is for the school to hire one teacher to teach all of the classes in the grade for each subject. This model is easy to implement and minimizes the number of lessons that each teacher needs to plan. This is how the model looks on a schedule:

| 9th Grade Instructional Schedule | | | | |
|---|---|---|---|---|
| | **English** | **History** | **Math** | **Science** |
| **Period 1** | Anderson | Barnes | Charles | Dillon |
| **Period 2** | Anderson | Barnes | Charles | Dillon |
| **Period 3** | Anderson | Barnes | Charles | Dillon |
| **Period 4** | Anderson | Barnes | Charles | Dillon |

Unfortunately, the model's best attribute—its simplicity—takes away the richest of opportunities for adult learning. It fosters isolation. All teachers are teaching a course *by themselves*, and therefore, no teacher needs or wants to regularly share lesson plans with any other teacher. The school might create other types of meetings that teachers attend— teachers might collaborate on an occasional interdisciplinary project or engage in weekly departmental planning meetings. But, as we explained earlier, the Artisan Teaching model is based on a premise that teachers should collaborate in the most important, daily work of all teachers: writing their curriculum and delivering their daily instruction. In this one-teacher-per-grade model, there is no opportunity for this type of authentic collaboration around the real work that teachers do every day. Just ask teachers what they want to talk about each day; in our experience, 95 percent of them want to have smart conversations every day with colleagues on how to best teach the next day's (or the next unit's) lessons. Any successful school organization must organize around this dominant adult need/want.

At AMS, the school leaders deliberately created structures that would allow a small school to have more than one teacher in each grade/subject, thereby creating collaborative teams. These structures are deliberately not the most efficient. But what is lost through inefficiency is more than made up for in the opportunities for adult learning. It's a trade-off that lies at the heart of the model's success.

Many strategies allow this model to function, and small schools can implement a variety of them across different grade levels.

## Block Scheduling

In this model, schools can use block scheduling to provide double-period blocks that incorporate two subject areas into one class with one teacher. This allows for two teachers to share a curriculum, even with the same number of students shared equally. AMS uses this model in middle school, by providing the students with two "core academic" classes: Humanities (English and social studies together in one course) and Math/Science (together in one course). This approach allows teams to be created as follows:

| 6th Grade Instructional Schedule | | | | |
|---|---|---|---|---|
| | Humanities | Humanities | Math/ Science | Math/ Science |
| Periods 1 & 2 | Anderson | Barnes | Charles | Dillon |
| Periods 3 & 4 | Anderson | Barnes | Charles | Dillon |

Using this model, students have a double period of humanities and math/science every day, and teacher Anderson teaches two double periods of humanities (instead of four single periods of English). Teacher Barnes also teaches two double periods of humanities, allowing Anderson and Barnes to form a team and collaborate on their daily lesson plans. The same is done for math and science classes, which become one course with a single teacher for a double period.

## Team Leaders with Split Assignments

In this model, the role of Team Leader is used to create teams. Because the TL is a highly successful veteran teacher with a reduced teaching assignment, it is often particularly effective (and strategic) for the TL to teach a "split" assignment—that is, teaching fewer sections, but also teaching two different courses. For example, in this teaching assignment model, Team Leader Thompson teaches only two classes per day, one of 9th grade English and one of 10th grade English. This allows her to serve as the TL for both courses and to work with the less experienced teachers on those teams. (And, although she has two "preps," the team model allows her to share the work of lesson planning with two other teachers.)

| 9th Grade Instructional Schedule | | | | |
|---|---|---|---|---|
| | English | History | Math | Science |
| Period 1 | Anderson | | | |
| Period 2 | Anderson | | | |
| Period 3 | Anderson | | | |
| Period 4 | TL-Thompson | | | |
| 10th Grade Instructional Schedule | | | | |
| | English | History | Math | Science |
| Period 1 | Smith | | | |
| Period 2 | Smith | | | |
| Period 3 | Smith | | | |
| Period 4 | TL-Thompson | | | |

Using this model, both Anderson and Smith are supported by the Artisan Teaching apprenticeship model, with a veteran TL supporting them, while the TL also teaches a section of those courses. Because these teams exist, the TL is not merely a mentor but, rather, a true collaborator because she is one of the teachers of those grades and shares the daily lessons that they cocreate.

Of course, one might ask, "How can a school afford to hire three teachers for 9th and 10th grade English, instead of two?" The budgetary cost of this setup is not large, because both of the two teachers (Anderson and Smith) can fill another role during their fourth period now that Thompson is teaching those two sections. Anderson and Smith, for example, could each teach another class elsewhere in the school—perhaps an elective course in an area of their interest, or a daily advisory class. Alternatively, they might fill one of the reduced teaching assignment roles that the school needs (e.g., testing, programming, lunch duty, substitute teaching, or many others). In other words, this model does not add new teachers that the school needs to hire; rather, it merely requires the school leaders to reorganize the roles creatively among the available staff.

## School Leaders Teaching One Class

Another solution for small schools that normally would have one teacher teaching all sections of a course is for a school leader to teach one section of the class. This new teacher could be an assistant principal, staff developer, coach, or anyone who is serving as an instructional leader in the Artisan Teaching model. As discussed earlier, the model is designed so that instructional leaders spend more time working with a smaller number of teacher-teams—and by doing so, it is often logical for the leader to teach one class, as a part of this intensive work with that team.

| 9th Grade Instructional Schedule | | | | |
|---|---|---|---|---|
| | English | History | Math | Science |
| Period 1 | | | Charles | |
| Period 2 | | | Charles | |
| Period 3 | | | Charles | |
| Period 4 | | | Asst. Principal Jordan | |

## Special Education Teachers Included on Core Teams

Finally, another valuable method for creating Artisan Teaching teams, especially in small schools, is to include teachers of students with disabilities on the core academic teams. By doing so, the school simultaneously achieves two goals: (1) creating an Artisan Teaching team and (2) improving the collaboration and planning for students with disabilities.

Although special education rules and structures vary state by state, the difficulty of creating time for collaboration between general education and special education teachers is a well-documented problem. Many schools hire special education teachers to provide support for all students with disabilities on a particular grade level—requiring them to teach multiple subjects with little involvement in planning the lessons. We suggest that teachers of students with disabilities can be given a teaching assignment that fits the Artisan Teaching model, thereby including them as a full member of a planning team. Sometimes, if permitted, the teacher might want to teach one period per day in a general education classroom, or the school might employ teachers who are dually licensed both in special education and a specific content area. The school might also include a "team teaching" class, depending on the students' Individualized Education Plans (IEPs).

| 9th Grade Instructional Schedule | | | | |
|---|---|---|---|---|
| | **English** | **History** | **Math** | **Science** |
| **Period 1** | Anderson | | | |
| **Period 2** | Anderson | | | |
| **Period 3** | Anderson & Brown (special ed team teaching class) | | | |
| **Period 4** | Brown (special ed class or dual-licensed teacher with one general ed class) | | | |

In this example, Anderson is a 9th grade English teacher. Brown is a special education teacher, who might have a dual license in teaching English. One of their classes is a cotaught team teaching class, and Brown teaches one class by himself. In this scenario, Brown might be the Team Leader, or he might fill the remainder of his schedule with other assignments (e.g., small-group work with special education students, writing IEPs). The point is that the Artisan Teaching model provides us with an opportunity to incorporate the teacher of students with disabilities into the daily collaboration that is crucial for teacher and leader development. This approach improves the quality of instruction for students with disabilities (and general education students), by including special education and differentiation strategies into every lesson for the entire grade. It allows true collaborative planning time for teachers who are working with a team teaching class. Finally, it incorporates special ed instruction into all of the instructional discussions throughout the school.

## Chapter 6

**Question:** *I understand the idea of shifting leadership roles to match the Artisan Teaching approach, but I am still struggling to see any feasible way to provide this level of support for every teacher in my school. My leadership team barely has enough time to handle all the district compliance mandates and visit a few classrooms—how can we realistically add daily team meetings and classroom support with this level of intensity?*

**Answer:** The implementation of the Artisan Teaching approach requires a change in mindset about leadership roles. Of course, there isn't endless time in the day. Educators work incredibly hard—there is no way to add more work to our schedules, and we would never suggest that we should.

In our opinion, school leaders need to reassess how we spend our time and consider whether our work with 20, 30, or 50 teachers is working. Can we really transform a school by providing such a trivial amount of support for a large number of teachers? If not, our role needs to change. We are not suggesting that we *add* yet another role (serving as a Team Leader for a small group of teachers). Rather, we are suggesting that one leader's work with 50 teachers should stop—and we should replace that work with a different type of work with only five teachers at a time. The goal must be for school leaders to find those roles that are being done in a large-scale (and small-impact) way, eliminate that work, and reorganize our roles to do the same work within a real, collaborative team. When all of the roles are merged into that small-group structure, real transformation of a school can result.

# 7

Implementation Strategies:
Where to Start?

The Artisan Teaching model focuses on the deliberate and long-term development of teachers and leaders within the school. It requires deep, intensive support for teachers for several years, and it eschews the tendency toward "quick-fix" and "checklist" strategies for school reform. Nevertheless, the model is also flexible in its implementation—it can be started in any type of school and at any scale. It can be implemented schoolwide or, initially, with only a single team. And although a phase-in process will continue over the course of years, the Artisan Teaching model can have a significant impact on student achievement very quickly.

## Considering Capacity and Leverage

Before implementing the Artisan Teaching model, a school leader should consider the existing capacity within the school for initial Team Leaders. As described in Chapter 1, the leader must begin with a powerful vision of the school's beliefs about great teaching, and that vision may be articulated by one, two, or more initial leaders. The school leader must consider how many of those leaders already demonstrate mastery of the four elements of expertise: (1) academic content, (2) pedagogy, (3) youth development, and (4) adult development and internal locus of control. And the school leader must determine how many of these leaders can reorganize their schedules (as described in Chapter 6) to create the time required to lead collaborative teams on a daily basis. This core group makes up the school's initial Team Leaders.

The next steps depend on the number of available Team Leaders, the size of the school, the relative strength and weakness of instructional areas, and the areas where the school must show quick, significant achievement gains. With all of these factors in mind, the leader can select from various implementation methods. If a school begins with only a single Team Leader, say, with expertise in 11th grade U.S. history, the school can begin with one Artisan Teaching team and phase in from that point. If a school has a single Team Leader with expertise in math instruction, the school might choose to target the most problematic area of student achievement—say, 8th grade math—hoping to provide immediate improvement in the area where achievement results are lowest, and then phase in from that point. Another school may choose to implement the Artisan Teaching model immediately schoolwide. There is no need to rush the implementation to a schoolwide model—it is most important to guarantee that the initial Team Leaders have the expertise and time available for this new work. The long-term success of the model will depend not on the initial size of the Team Leader corps but on the success of the initial Team Leaders in *doubling the number of Team Leaders within three years.*

## Starting Small: Vertical Phase-In by Subject Area

The most likely scenario for an existing school leader is to pilot the Artisan Teaching model with one or two initial Team Leaders. If a school chooses to begin with a single Team Leader who has expertise in teaching 9th grade history, the school might choose a gradual phase-in of the model beginning only with the 9th grade history team. That team can begin functioning immediately using the model while the rest of the school continues functioning as it did previously. The apprenticeship work can be accomplished using any of the time allocation methods described in Chapter 6. If the initial Team Leader is an assistant principal (AP), that AP can be reassigned to provide support only for the two teachers on the 9th grade history team, and another administrator can take some of his or her other duties. If the Team Leader is a full-time history teacher, the school can provide one period of reduced teaching assignment in order to complete the role of the Team Leader.

Over the next few years, the existing Team Leader could take on another grade-level team ("vertically") within the history department. The instructional work of the members of the teams could expand department-wide with more teachers gradually joining apprenticeships over the first few years. As the work succeeds and teachers are supported with the intense mentoring that the model provides, soon a new Team Leader will emerge from within the high school history department. These two Team Leaders will provide leadership for the 9th, 10th, 11th, and 12th grade history teams, and all of the high school history teachers will be enveloped within the Artisan Teaching model.

The vertical phase-in of the model is helpful and appropriate for many common situations and provides many advantages:

- One initial Team Leader can begin with a manageable role.
- The school leader can deliberately target one grade/subject that requires quick improvement in student achievement results, allowing the initial Team Leader to have an immediate impact on achievement by supporting that team with intensive daily mentoring and teamwork.
- If a school leader is hoping to improve the curriculum and lesson planning (or implement new instructional materials or assessments), a vertical phase-in within a department can be particularly helpful. The school can begin the implementation with the youngest grade level in the school and "move up" each year with that cohort of students. This approach can provide consistency for a new instructional initiative or curriculum.
- If a single subject-area grade team faces the departure of a veteran teacher or an influx of brand-new teachers who will need substantial and intensive support, the school leader may see great benefit from implementing the model initially with that team. For example, two new first-year teachers could be assigned to fill

the gap of a veteran departure, and the assistant principal Team Leader could work initially with that one team, simultaneously filling a need for intensive mentoring and phasing in the model.

## Horizontal Phase-In by Grade Level

Suppose another school has one or two initial Team Leaders and chooses to begin the Artisan Teaching model with only the 6th grade English team. After one year, the school might decide to phase-in the model by expanding it within the 6th grade, adding team leaders for 6th grade social studies, math, and science, for example.

Again, there are situations where a horizontal phase-in is a logical fit for a particular school. Horizontal phase-in provides advantages for schools in situations such as these:

- If the school has only a few initial Team Leaders, with expertise in different subject areas—one English teacher and one math teacher, for example—then it might be logical to assign them to the same grade.
- For programming reasons, one entire grade might have a "common prep" at the same time. For example, if the entire 6th grade has physical education for 60 minutes after lunch, then all of the 6th grade teachers (except the PE teachers) could be available for team planning meetings during that period. Therefore, incorporating the whole 6th grade into the model might prove to be very efficient.
- If one leader provides support for a grade level (and is responsible in a supervisory role for all subject areas in that grade), such as an assistant principal for the 5th grade, that leader might choose to implement the model horizontally across that grade level.
- In lower grade levels, such as elementary school, a horizontal implementation of the model might be effective where the teachers teach a wider range of subjects. If a small number of

teachers are responsible for the entire 3rd grade—because each teacher teaches English, social studies, and science—the horizontal implementation of the Artisan Teaching model will assist those teachers by supporting the lesson planning across the entire grade. Those teachers might benefit greatly from the collaboration with other teachers on the same grade level, each of whom might have different areas of instructional strength.

## Combination/Flexible Implementation

One advantage of the Artisan Teaching model is its flexibility—starting slowly and implementing in specific grades or subject areas is logical and effective. It is also necessary, however, for the school leaders to maintain flexibility during phase-in. School leaders must maintain fidelity to the vision and mission of the model, which requires them to assign a Team Leader to a new role only when that Team Leader is ready and well suited for the new assignment. With that in mind, it may be impossible to predict the most logical direction or pace of implementation across a school.

For example, consider a school that implements the Artisan Teaching model with one Team Leader for 9th grade English and another for 11th grade math, assuming that those are the areas of expertise for the two initial Team Leaders. The school leaders will hope and expect that after two or three years of work with collaborative teams, a few new prospective Team Leaders will emerge. This process is gradual and follows the long-term development of the teachers on those teams. Perhaps another one of the 9th grade English teachers and one of the 11th grade math teachers become the school's next two Team Leaders (the third and fourth Team Leaders). Suppose the new 9th grade Team Leader is an artisan English teacher who excitedly asks to move to 10th grade, where she can help *another team* write new curriculum and improve instruction. Perhaps she has earned great respect among the 10th grade English teachers, and those teachers welcome her support. In this case, the school leader logically might move that teacher to the 10th grade for the following year. She will bring a deep knowledge of the students who move with her from 9th to 10th grade, and this shift will allow a vertical phase-in of the model within the English department, with Team Leaders in both 9th and 10th grades.

Alternatively, the new team leader who taught 11th grade math might have a different goal. The 11th grade math teacher, hypothetically, might have been a physics major in college and could have a deep interest in continuing to teach 11th grade math. The principal might decide that this teacher should serve as the Team Leader for 11th grade math and 11th grade physics, where she can provide expertise across a grade level. The principal might see a reflective, inexperienced physics teacher in the 11th grade who would benefit greatly from the support of the Artisan Teaching model. She might hope to implement interdisciplinary instructional projects that are coplanned between the math and science teachers, and the principal might therefore encourage a horizontal phase-in of the model in the 11th grade.

The point is that the successful implementation of the Artisan Teaching model—like so many things inside schools—can be highly personalized and individualized, and depends on the various strengths, expertise, and personal choices of the teachers and leaders involved in the decisions. The Team Leader assignments can, and should, be considered with deep understanding of the teachers and leaders available. School leaders should weight the various strengths and weaknesses of the teachers and Team Leaders, and they should determine which partnerships are more (or less) likely to succeed. These considerations may often be more important than a preconceived plan for the implementation of the model, and these individualized issues might convince the school leader to adjust the Team Leader assignments in any given year.

## Iteration and Exponential Spread Throughout the School

The key aspect of any phase-in approach of the Artisan Teaching model is *iteration*. That is, after the initial Team Leaders have been identified, with each team composed of two to three teachers and the TL, we find that it takes, on average, two to three years to "graduate" the next TL from the original group of two to three team members. After the two to three years, the model iterates; after an additional two to three years, it iterates yet again. This process means the number of team leaders grows exponentially every two to three years.

The following graphic illustrates the exponential growth of team leaders. Suppose that a school starts with just three teams, two led by "TL-A" and one led by "TL-B." To start, teachers A1, A2, and A3 are on one of TL-A's teams. Teachers A4, A5, and A6 are on TL-A's other team. Teachers B1, B2, and B3 are on TL-B's team. The phase-in process looks like this:

| TL-A | TL-A | TL-B |
|---|---|---|
| A1 A2 A3 | A4 A5 A6 | B1 B2 B3 |

In the model, on average, one TL emerges from each team of two to three teachers during the course of two to three years. Suppose that in the starting scenario above, that after two to three years Al, A4, and B1 are the teachers who become future TLs. Then after two to three years, the school retains the three teams led by A and B and also generates three additional teams led by A1, A4, and B1. This is the first iteration (or "second generation"):

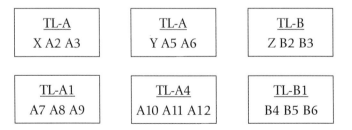

| TL-A | TL-A | TL-B |
|---|---|---|
| X A2 A3 | Y A5 A6 | Z B2 B3 |

| TL-A1 | TL-A4 | TL-B1 |
|---|---|---|
| A7 A8 A9 | A10 A11 A12 | B4 B5 B6 |

Note that after a period of two to three years, the number of initial collaborative teams has *doubled*. Similarly, after four to six years, iteration has occurred and the number of teams doubles yet again to 12.

The growth of team leaders in this process is *exponential*—with an exponentially growing number of instructional leaders in the school, and an ever-increasing number of teachers receiving the intensive support of a TL within the apprenticeship model. Mathematically, the iteration process embedded within Artisan Teaching looks like this:

Number of teams = $(s)2^n$
  $s$ = number of initial teams
  $n$ = number of two- to three-year iterations

## Chapter 7

**Question:** *It sounds like you are suggesting a model for improving schools that will take a long time. I'm under real pressure and need to demonstrate improvement quickly. How can the Artisan Teaching approach help me?*

**Answer:** Getting good results in a timely fashion and developing artisan teachers (who then get good data later on) are not mutually exclusive. While overhauling an entire school toward the Artisan Teaching approach does take time, real, measurable changes can be seen in the middle of the first iteration. To be sure, we are suggesting an approach that requires sustained and intensive work over a long period of time. However, with any one team, the results can be dramatic and quick.

At the heart of the approach is this premise: instead of trying to make a large number of teachers each a little bit better, the new model concentrates the work intensely on one grade with one subject. Those in the Artisan Teaching model will show much larger gains than those in a traditional model. And the model can be a turbo boost to student achievement by targeting the team with the most depressed results, impacting the school's aggregated data substantially and almost immediately. A failing high school with underachieving data in 9th grade algebra, for example, could begin the Artisan Teaching approach only with 9th grade algebra. By targeting the highest-need areas first, the model leverages the school's instructional leadership capacity to improve achievement results more quickly.

After targeting the areas in most need, data will improve by the first year. By the time of the middle of the second iteration (year 3 or 4), the number of teams has doubled, and substantial results can be seen in a large part of the school.

# 8

## Strategies for Hiring

One of the most common laments we hear from school leaders is that that there are so few great teachers available to hire. We agree, and that's why we don't try to look for great teachers or even proficient ones. In our experience, most proficient teachers have parlayed their skills into desirable teaching assignments and are already held in high regard by both colleagues and supervisors at their current schools. This leaves little incentive to search for a similar new job, earning essentially the same salary, at a different school. From a school leader's perspective, it is a losing proposition to try to find excellent teachers and convince them to leave the school where they have had success and somehow, without any significant additional money, lure them to a new school.

Given the hiring realities just described, a next logical attempt might be to try hire the best teachers one can find, even if these teachers are not yet great but merely, say, proficient. Or, put another way, assuming a continuum of teacher proficiency starting with *new*, moving to *proficient*, and eventually landing on *great*, many leaders assume that hiring proficient teachers is the best way to develop great teachers, because they are further along the continuum. We reject that logic. We believe that current placement along the proficiency continuum is not relevant to the potential to become great.

The hiring process necessary to support the Artisan Teaching model requires great discipline and tremendous focus of hiring managers. In particular, *hiring managers must not confuse proficiency with potential,* and we must not allow ourselves to be distracted by proficiency when greatness is the goal. Moreover, if proficiency is no longer the name of the hiring game, then what is? What *are* the reliable predictors of artisanship teaching, and what activities and methods can be developed that will reveal a candidate's potential? These are the questions answered in this chapter.

---

**DIARY OF A TEACHER**
**Job Interview**

*Going into my interview, I was feeling well prepared. I had previously talked to friends who had interviewed at other schools and found out the most frequently asked questions. I prepared answers to those questions and even role-played with a friend from college. I had a demonstration lesson all set, was sure to call students "scholars," was going to mention "the rigors of the Common Core," and say that I will "use data to drive instruction."*

*Boy, was I wrong! Yes, I did teach a lesson, and I thought it went pretty well. But I was definitely not prepared for what occurred. They sat and talked to me for a long time afterward, asking me to justify every part of my lesson. Why would kids care about my lesson? How did I get kids to think deeply and not just identify terms? About 30 minutes in, I fully realized that my lesson hadn't come close to the mark. But then something really cool happened: we started to rebuild the lesson. When I stumbled, they helped, but it was definitely on me to think my way through this; they would not move on until I suggested good changes to the lesson, and they would not move on until I could explain why the changes would help. It was at times frustrating but it was also fun. For almost three hours I was thinking about thinking, and I felt something I had not yet felt before: on the spot, I was becoming a better teacher. That's what I want from a school!*

It should be noted that it is not that we refuse to hire teachers who are already excellent (sometimes we do); it is that this event is such a rarity that we cannot build a staffing plan around it. One of the keys to staffing in the Artisan Teaching model is that hiring does not depend on finding excellent teachers, which opens up the domain for where to search. While this approach offers more candidates, it also means we need to look at way more candidates to get the ones we want and that we must have an effective, efficient process from résumé acquisition to eventual hire. Over 12 years of hiring teachers, we have refined, tracked, and formalized our hiring process. We have identified clearly desired candidate traits (e.g., reflectiveness), identified alluring but distracting indicators (e.g., proficiency), and constructed a five-stage process with associated activities and key indicators that determine how candidates progress through the stages (Figure 8.1).

Note that one efficiency that can be gained in the five-stage process is through the efficient use of teacher hiring fairs. If minimal time is spent on candidates who certainly will not be hired, and if interviewers have mastered phone-interview skills, then we have found that it is possible to combine Stages 1 and 2 at the fair, eliminating the phone interview entirely. However, this "shortcut" is not easy to do and, if not done well, will generate many "false positives," resulting in scheduling demo lessons for candidates inappropriately. Overscheduling demos must be avoided due to the time investment by leaders and the disruption to regular instruction. We would encourage this practice (going from hiring fair to demo lesson) only after the school has refined the phone interview sufficiently. To start, schools should use the hiring fair as additional info to determine who will get phone interviews.

Hiring well for this model is labor intensive, taking approximately 27 hours of high-level aggregated school effort to secure one teacher (see Figure 8.1). If the school has a significant number of teaching vacancies, then hiring needs to become a large portion of leaders' jobs during hiring season (typically April to July). Although, as we explain later, moving from stage 3 to stage 4 requires the deepest level of skill from the interviewers, all stage movements are critical.

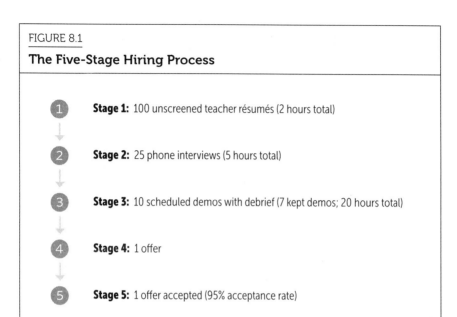

FIGURE 8.1

**The Five-Stage Hiring Process**

**Stage 1:** 100 unscreened teacher résumés (2 hours total)

**Stage 2:** 25 phone interviews (5 hours total)

**Stage 3:** 10 scheduled demos with debrief (7 kept demos; 20 hours total)

**Stage 4:** 1 offer

**Stage 5:** 1 offer accepted (95% acceptance rate)

Movement from Stage 1 to Stage 2 requires the culling of résumés at the rate of roughly 4:1. Stage 1 → Stage 2 "Résumé Screening" is elimination work, rejecting résumés without benefit of a phone conversation. Red flags include poorly written, cliché-filled résumés, employment history of jumping from job to job, outsized and preposterous claims of achievement, missing appropriate state license, and the inclusion of significant amounts of irrelevant detail. The critical thing here is to eliminate résumés so that the funnel does not clog at the next step.

To successfully move from Stage 2 to Stage 3, candidates need to pass a phone interview. Again, this step is crucial in the "winnowing" process, to guarantee that only qualified candidates reach the next stage. Successful candidates will be able to speak smartly about themselves and their motivation for teaching, avoiding clichés and jargon. They should be able to describe in good detail one of their favorite academic classes that they have ever been a part of (as a teacher or as a learner) and, without prompting, link their enjoyment to the way the teacher made the students *think* in new ways—not because they achieved a high test score or earned a good grade. They should talk more about poetry or the Pythagorean theorem than about data. In fact, they do not need to mention "Common Core," "data," or "no-excuse" policies at all.

When asked about classroom behavior, we hope that potential candidates talk about teacher consistency, the teacher making connections with students, and the teacher coming off as "believable." It is not helpful (to them) if they talk about discipline systems, deans, or other school personnel. In the initial phone conversation, they articulate, through response to scenarios, a strong internal locus of control. They can speak fondly and authentically of being part of a team at some point in their lives. If they have had a coach or mentor who has helped them, they characterize this coach as inspirational and uncompromising in quality. They come off as sharp people who are able to understand, make connections, and articulate nontrivial ideas well. Those who pass the phone interview can speak about themes in core academic subjects (have sufficient content knowledge) and do so with appropriate fluency, insight, and enthusiasm.

## Actionable Reflectiveness

The most important trait (and the one that carries the weight of our final hiring decisions) that we seek in the demo/debrief process is what we refer to as *actionable reflectiveness*, to underscore that we do not mean passive agreeability, general openness, or even the willingness to accept criticism; rather, we mean an active, helpful disposition during both lesson revision and lesson creation processes that leads to practical, observable, and implementable improvement. It is a tendency and even an enthusiasm for self-criticism along with the ability to transform this self-criticism quickly into significant actionable improvement within the Artisan Teaching model.

This quality is, we believe, by far the single biggest indicator toward developing into a great teacher. Those who are reflective in this way are quick to criticize themselves and do so openly—even in a job interview when many people try to hide their faults. But actionably reflective people also maintain a positive disposition when they are being self-critical, because they are not angry about their imperfections; rather, they are excited about the prospect of improving their work. Reflective individuals do not become defensive in the face of criticism, because they do not view their mistakes as something to fear or defend. The truly reflective candidates assume, quite naturally, that the ability to discover and correct their imperfections is a fun challenge that is necessary to push their work to excellent. They embrace authentic criticism without hesitation.

Moving from Stage 3 to Stage 4 requires that the candidate perform a teaching "demo lesson" and participate directly afterward in a debrief of that lesson. This demo/debrief is the most critical part of the hiring process and the most time consuming. It is where we test for the key quality of *reflectiveness* and, in particular, the ability to receive feedback in a team-based format and *immediately translate that feedback into improvement*. Reflectiveness in this context is the single biggest indicator of potential for accelerated adult growth and by far the best predictor we have found of future artisan teaching.

But how can you reliably check for reflectiveness and ability to improve from authentic teamwork? Asking candidates to share a time when they demonstrated reflectiveness or if they are "team players" will reveal nothing, in our opinion. Of course people will say they are reflective and team players. The interviewers would have no idea if the candidates are portraying their scenarios and their dispositions accurately. Are their stories of being on a team true or fabricated on the spot to impress? Moreover, access to standard interview questions—including ones about reflectiveness—is so widespread that most candidates can predict the standard questions and even role-play these questions ahead of time. To us, there is no point asking any of these well-anticipated questions.

☛ **TIP 1 FOR INTERVIEWING**

**Interviewers need to be artisan teachers trained to the task.**

*Conducting an effective debrief is difficult, and the school must have at least one person to serve as a model who can train others. This interviewer must be able to observe a lesson of any proficiency level and on the spot, individually if need be, dismantle it, find the major shortcomings, and then reconstruct this lesson so that it is superb. There is no way that a merely proficient teacher can do this. Even an artisan teacher needs to be trained to do this well. And if no such interviewer exists, then the school needs to get someone trained to do it. Bonus points if the interviewer is the principal.*

We believe strongly that the only way to determine the ability to take criticism and show reflectiveness is to deliberately critique the candidate and evaluate the response for indicators of reflectiveness (or for indicators of a lack thereof). Of course the candidate wants to teach well, but from the school's perspective, the teacher demonstration then is definitely not a showcase in which to gauge proficiency. This can be quite counterintuitive, necessitating that hiring managers remain disciplined and not conflate the ideas of proficiency and potential as evidenced by reflectiveness. If proficiency is the goal, then the interviewer naturally will focus in a demo lesson on the quality of the lesson. If reflectiveness is the goal, the interviewer acts and thinks differently—the quality of the lesson is less important, and the interviewer focuses much more intently on the candidate's response to criticism during the debrief.

For us, the demonstration lesson is merely material for discussion, allowing interviewers to challenge choices made. It is crucial, therefore, for the prospective teacher to write their own lesson plan for the demonstration lesson (and not to teach one of the school's lessons), in order to allow an authentic discussion afterward about the decisions and thought process that went into the lesson plan. Although we have found that 30 to 40 minutes of demonstration teaching is enough to generate sufficient material (candidate choices) for effective debrief, the length of the debrief varies between 20 minutes (candidate is not a good fit) to four hours (debrief goes so well that no one wants it to end, and the candidate leaves with a job offer). And although there is no prepared set of questions (except the open-ended "Why did you choose this lesson to teach?"), we consistently press two key themes, *student interest* and *higher-order thinking,* and we use the lens of *intentionality of teacher choices made*.

By driving questions in these directions with increasing levels of depth, either reflectiveness will begin to emerge or, in some cases, the candidate begins to show signs of defensiveness or evasion. It should be noted that this technique requires substantial interviewer discipline and a tolerance for awkward periods of silence to deliberately push the candidate, organically and contextually, past his or her knowledge and skill level. It may feel awkward for candidate and interviewers alike, but the interviewer must not cave to the desire to ease the awkwardness. The candidate needs to think his or her way through the silence.

---

**☞ TIP 2 FOR INTERVIEWING**
**Don't fear or fill the silences.**

*Regardless of how proficient the demo lesson, there will be necessary periods of awkward silence and tension during the debrief of the lesson. Also, since this type of interview is new for them, give the candidate thinking time. Do not be afraid of long pauses as they think during the discussion. Do not fill in that thinking time with commentary or try to ease the tension through talk. Make it safe for the candidate to think.*

Our goal is not to make the candidate feel good, feel bad, or feel any way in particular. We do believe, however, in harnessing the power of emotional tension, a term Peter Senge (2006) defined and used in his work *The Fifth Discipline*. Senge argues that emotional tension—the feelings associated with a significant gap between the current state of affairs and a desired state of affairs—needs to be managed adroitly by leaders in order to ensure that the current state moves toward the desired state and not vice versa. In particular, Senge suggests that leaders must embrace this tension and resist the urge to eliminate it. In our context, the great interviewers go into the debrief knowing that it is their job as interviewers to create tension by revealing a gap between current teacher performance and the desired state of teacher performance. What will *the interviewer* do with this tension? The interviewer must not demoralize the candidate and needs to reveal just the right parts of the gap so that the candidate, if predisposed, will wade into the tension and push the lesson and himself or herself toward excellence.

Of course the demo debrief can be characterized as a hiring structure that surfaces reflectiveness, but it can also be regarded as a preview of the candidate as a member of a collaborative team meeting. The Artisan Teaching model requires us to hire teachers who will engage and succeed in the work of collaboratively discussing curriculum and instruction, because this is the heart of the work using the model. With that in mind, the demo lesson debrief is most certainly not scripted, nor can it be pulled off through a prepared sequence of questions. Instead, we ask the candidates to reflect on the spot on what they just did. Doing so requires that the interviewers be able to dive deep, instructionally, into any demo lesson presented, just as they would push a teacher on their teams, as well as a degree of improvisation by the interviewer.

The interviewers should focus on the intentionality of choices made: *Why did you choose to have students read the paragraph first? Why did you have students read silently and work alone? What could you have done differently? Approximately what percent of students were engaged during this activity, and how do you know? When you pointed to that equation, what happened to student thinking? Why did you not approach the students who were off task? What thinking—what connections, what inferences, what deductions—did students have to do in order to answer your question? Where did this lesson get hard for students? During what period did they think critically, and why do you say that? What part of the task that you chose requires higher-order thinking? How could you have gotten them to engage in more higher-order thinking? Instead of saying, "Let's factor  x2 + 3x + 2," how can you motivate students to genuinely want to factor this expression?*

---

☞ **TIP 3 FOR INTERVIEWING**
**Minimize the potential shock value of the process.**

*Do not confuse a candidate's apparent lack of reflectiveness with the initial shock of a candidate going through this process. The candidate most likely has not faced questions so pointed and that speak so directly to the effectiveness of their decisions. We have found that the technique of trying to make a candidate better during the debrief is almost always awkward at first and, in any event, a jarring contrast to what most candidates expect to happen at an interview. Candidates most likely expect to be asked standard interview questions readily available from a variety of sources. However, they cannot prepare for* "When you asked that question, no one responded. Why do you think that is, and what could you have done differently?" *Therefore, it is important to be explicit at the beginning that there are no standard interview questions and the focus is on the lesson just taught.*

---

In almost all demo lessons (especially with new teachers), there is a definite lack of student interest and higher-order thinking, something that, as we mentioned earlier, we expect. The question is, how quickly does the candidate acknowledge this and to what extent does the candidate, with our help, make the lesson substantially better? If the teacher is not reflective, by the 20-minute mark, it will start to become apparent. The candidate will be unable or unwilling to accept an accurate picture of the classroom. Or he or she may see the lack in the lesson but be unable to come up with alternative approaches or activities that would generate better results. If given help in coming up with better ideas for tasks, the candidate will be unable to explain why they are better and will be unsuccessful at fleshing out those ideas into actual directions for students and the teacher.

Interviewers need to manage the clock well here. To see if it will turn around, the interviewers may continue for another 10 minutes and can even give the candidate, say, a good idea for a more thought-provoking activity. However, if the candidate still is not leaning into the conversation with his or her own contributions after 30 minutes, it is time to call it. The balance for the interviewers is to give enough time to ensure that this candidate does not become a false negative, while also not spending unnecessary time on someone who you are not going to hire. Until this point. you have already made a substantial investment in this candidate—a phone interview, at least two school leaders watched a demo lesson, and then these two leaders joined the demo debrief. That aggregates to approximately five hours of time. A this point, the leaders need to be okay with ending the interview.

On the other hand, reflective teachers seem to readily agree with the deconstruction of the lesson at about the 20-minute mark, and the best of them, without prompting, are already starting to think about what they could have done differently. These teachers relish the idea of helping to reconstruct the lesson so that it is of much higher quality. Although there is no script for doing so, the general idea is to reconstruct the lesson to the highest standard possible while giving the candidate— the indicator of a great debrief is a fully reconstructed lesson that meets the highest bar for excellence with substantial input from the candidate.

And when the debrief turns the corner at the 20- to 30-minute mark and during the next two hours the candidate greatly contributes and enjoys a difficult conversation that pushes towards excellence, an inescapably emotional experience has occurred. We believe this emotion is the reason that the vast majority of candidates offered employment at AMS choose to accept their offers. By the end of the four-hour total experience, the candidate has been frustrated, challenged, helped, challenged more, and improved. Not just the lesson, but the candidate's thinking and understanding of quality and excellence have come into sharper focus. The interview itself, consisting of the demo and debrief, has been a challenging but significant learning experience for the candidate. At this point, we don't have to tell the candidate what support looks like in our school—they just experienced it.

---

☞ **TIP 4 FOR INTERVIEWING**

**For the demo lesson, the candidate should choose the subject and write his or her own plan.**

*One of the keys to the debrief process and why it is so effective is it focuses on the candidate's intentionality of choices. The process relies on having a wide range of candidate choices to explore later on during the debrief.*

*Make sure to tell candidates to create their own lesson. Downloaded, scripted lessons are unhelpful and tell the candidate as much. In fact, open it up in the other direction: tell the candidate that he or she can choose any topic in any academic subject. We do not want a candidate on a demo teaching a topic he or she is uncomfortable with (which would potentially adversely affect the ability to look for reflectivity). We want the teacher choosing a lesson, and then we want to hear why that choice was made. We want to hear that thinking. Also, do not ask the candidate to match the class's current pacing chart in an effort to not lose instructional time for students. This will not only restrict candidate choice, but the candidate likely won't teach it well, anyway! Remember: you need to observe choices made both prior to and during the lesson.*

---

Although the debrief is neither linear nor at times even clear (it depends much on the quality of the candidate), the decision whether to offer a candidate a position is straightforward. After the debrief, the following four conditions need to be met clearly:

- The candidate must have enjoyed the process; otherwise, he or she will not likely seek out these kinds of meetings.
- The interviewers must be able to say that the candidate is reflective and open.
- The interviewers must be able to say that the candidate contributed significantly to the process of rebuilding the lesson.
- The lesson must have been greatly improved. By "greatly improved," we mean if the candidate were to teach the lesson again and make the changes based on the meeting, students would be *significantly more engaged,* and the lesson would engender *significantly more higher-order thinking.*

Figures 8.2 and 8.3 illustrate, respectively, a traditional one-dimensional model of searching for the most proficient teachers, contrasted with a two-dimensional model that considers both a candidate's present proficiency and potential for future development—the Artisan Teaching model's approach to hiring.

FIGURE 8.2

## Traditional One-Dimensional Model
## for Analysis of Teaching Candidates

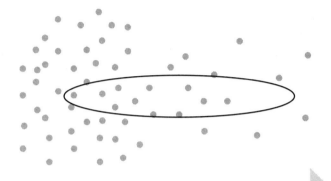

Analysis of Candidate's Current
Talent & Quality of Teaching

In this typical scenario, schools search for teachers of the highest possible quality and talent level. They spend their time and energy seeking teachers who are as far "to the right" as possible on the spectrum of current talent and quality. However, there are so few candidates on the right side of the graph—most are clustered toward the newer and lower stage of development; as a result, most of the teachers hired turn out to be far from artisan teachers. The school, inevitably, is faced with the task of helping those teachers develop into artisan teachers *after* they are hired.

FIGURE 8.3

## Two-Dimensional Model Focusing on Both Current Ability and the Expected Rate of Development

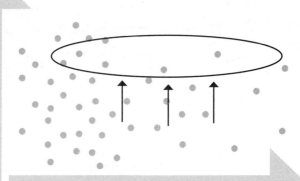

In the Artisan Teaching model, schools interview from the same pool of candidates and continue to seek the most talented and highest-quality teachers (looking for teachers on the right side of the graph).

In this scenario, however, the school uses an interview process designed to identify teachers who are higher up on the $y$-axis—that is, teachers who are more reflective and more likely to develop quickly within the Artisan Teaching model. By focusing on the qualities that are indicators of adult development (rather than only on the quality of teaching), the Artisan Teaching school shifts its group of new teachers upward, increasing the rate of development the teachers will have over the course of the next few years. As a result, although the group of teachers hired at the school is of the same quality (in year 1), these teachers are more likely to thrive in the apprenticeship model, more likely to embrace and seek critical feedback, and more likely to become Team Leaders a few years later. The teachers on the top left of the graph are new and inexperienced—but also very likely to become future instructional leaders, if provided the proper support. Teachers on the bottom left are less likely to do so.

## Chapter 8

**Question:** *What is the impact of the Artisan Teaching approach on teacher retention? What happens to the teachers who do not become Team Leaders? What does that do to staff morale and teacher attrition?*

**Answer:** First, it should be noted that minimizing teacher attrition is not a primary goal of the Artisan Teaching model. Some teachers do not want to become artisan teachers and may choose to pursue other career ambitions. Some teachers generally do not like feedback, do not like sharing ideas, and want to be largely left alone. These teachers are not a fit for a highly collaborative model, and they may choose a more appropriate school for them. Others may have a different view of great instruction than the Artisan Teaching school's leaders. Any of these preferences are legitimate, and it is not our goal to keep all of those teachers in a school that does not match their needs.

However, we believe that most teachers do like the idea of authentic collaboration, regardless of whether their careers head toward becoming a Team Leader. Even if a teacher does not progress toward TL status, a basic professional need is being met. That need is not to discuss data. That need is not having a yearlong series of training sessions after school on "accountable talk." Rather, teachers want to have productive conversations daily with a team about how to plan and deliver the most engaging, rigorous, and enjoyable lessons possible. Even those who do not make it to TL level are still experiencing the lifeblood of the school and enjoying and benefiting from it. They still feel strongly supported by their teammates. Not many people choose to leave jobs where they get this rapport with their colleagues.

Indeed, every school has teachers who earn promotions and new titles, and others who do not. Every profession faces this issue. The benefits of these opportunities (for new roles, job advancement opportunities, distributed leadership) far outweigh the difficulties.

# Epilogue
## How Did We Get Here?

Try this: find a few friends or relatives who have a variety of professional careers—not in education, and not brand new to their professions. Start with people who have been successful for some time and are proud of the work they do. Ask them how they became good at their jobs. With virtually every professional other than an educator, you will hear strikingly similar answers:

> I became great at my job because of my mentor. I worked on her team for the first two years. She taught me what to focus on and how to generate *my* best work. She helped me think through difficult issues, pushing me to produce work of much higher quality than I otherwise would have.

You will hear a lawyer, for example, explain that he worked on teams handling cases. The junior associate on the team wrote the first draft of the briefs, and a senior attorney edited it, rewrote parts thoroughly, and improved it substantially. Only then did the firm send the brief to the client and submit it to the court. All of the lawyers worked together, as a team, on the same brief before it was "done." The work was done as a team, with highly successful and talented veterans leading the newer lawyers.

You will hear a doctor who completed rounds at the hospital for several years, while the experienced doctors on her team corrected her mistakes and explained anything she did wrong, before she ever took a leadership role with patients. The physician assisted in hundreds of surgeries before she could ever handle a patient on her own.

You will hear an airline pilot explain that he learned how to be successful from his copilot, assisting on hundreds of flights before he became the lead pilot on a flight. A newspaper reporter who worked daily on articles with her first editor. An accountant who worked on a team. An electrician who apprenticed for three years before starting his own company.

And you'll certainly hear one more thing: "It took years of practice!" Virtually everyone who cares about their profession and respects their own work will describe the difficulty of becoming great at it: "I worked my way to the top for years!" "I apprenticed with John for three years until I really got it down." "My papers had more red ink from suggested edits for rewrite than my actual writing." "She edited everything I wrote for years until I got to be the writer I am today!" "Mary was an amazing mentor—she never stopped pushing me to get better." It takes years of hard work to develop greatness in a challenging field. It takes dedication and practice to become an artisan.

There are also some answers that you'll *never* hear from a highly talented professional, such as these:

- "I became great at my work by attending workshops or training sessions."
- "I became great at my work because my boss visited once a week for 15 minutes and then rated me with a rubric and gave me a next step."
- "I became great at my job by analyzing data measuring my results daily and weekly."

These answers represent the most common strategies schools are currently using to develop teachers, but they are not the strategies we use to develop adults in any other profession. Our country has millions of exceptional and successful lawyers, doctors, accountants, journalists, artists, musicians, electricians, and other professionals—and, without exaggeration, *none of them* developed greatness solely by participating in PD sessions, weekly data analysis meetings, or monthly formal observation feedback cycles. Yet, these are the dominant methods we use to develop great teachers.

Consider these strategies a bit more carefully. Other professions simply do not attempt to train their employees with workshops. "Professional development" sessions don't exist—training is always embedded in the actual work, while professionals are doing the actual work of their job. Of course, there are limited exceptions. A doctor might attend a training to learn how to use a new medical device, or a pilot might be trained on a simulator before flying a new plane. But these are targeted training sessions to provide specific content knowledge—training sessions are not considered to be the mechanism for the fundamental development of a professional. Bosses don't stay after work hours to teach employees lessons or conduct workshops. They stay after work to finish a project—that is, they just do their real work.

Consider observation-and-feedback cycles. Obviously, all professions have systems for evaluating and rating their employees. Doctors and lawyers are evaluated, promoted, and earn pay increases based on their performance. But in all other professions, these annual evaluations are done to provide information that will inform the employee of his or her status and areas for growth. They are *not* considered to be a central part of the employee's training. In professions other than education, the real training happens during the completion of the work itself.

Similarly, data analysis is important in many fields. We look at statistics of athletes, success rates of hospital procedures, and crime rates for local police precincts. But that work is done by central administrators to decide how to allocate funds and how to make big-picture changes within the institutions. Only in education is data analysis seen as something the employees themselves should do *to foster their own growth.* In other professions, we recognize that it doesn't work that way. Data are the *result* of great work, not a mechanism for improving it.

Indeed, the "data-driven instruction" movement is a particularly harmful trend in education. We believe data analysis is a practice that is misunderstood by educators and is obstructing real efforts to improve classroom teaching.

The New York City Police Department and the Oakland Athletics baseball team are both famous for their well-chronicled successes using data (see, e.g., Lewis, 2004; Zimring, 2013). The NYPD demonstrated unprecedented decreases in crime rates in the 1990s by analyzing precise, real-time crime data on a block-by-block basis. It allowed them to reallocate resources immediately to neighborhoods that needed additional support. The Oakland Athletics used sophisticated data analysis to determine what players would improve their team the most—and they won several World Series titles as a result.

But educators misunderstand the lessons of these other professions. The central offices of the NYPD and Oakland Athletics worked intensely to analyze numerical data and set targets for their improvement. Nobody would suggest, however, that NYPD officers should spend their time reviewing statistics to improve the quality of their own work. It would be comical to suggest that Oakland Athletics players should spend less time in batting practice and, instead, analyze their data and set SMART goals for their batting in the upcoming season. The work with data is done by central administrators to determine resource allocations, not as a tool to improve the work of individual professionals.

Similarly, it makes perfect sense for a school district to evaluate assessment data and to use it as a tool to evaluate the success of schools. Principals can certainly review assessment results to identify which classes or grade levels are achieving at higher rates. We are not opposed to the use of data by central administrators—we hope this information can serve the same valuable purpose it does for the NYPD. Data can *identify* stronger or weaker practices. But this data analysis has no place in the daily work of a teacher, because it is not a tool to help that teacher improve. Of course, all great teachers analyze their students' work every day, adjusting their instruction based on student understandings and the work they do in class. But the data movement has gone far beyond the work that great teachers do in their planning every day, and it is creating layers of additional work that distracts from the most important work.

The current trend in education is to talk constantly about the need to "use" data—pre-assessments, setting goals, interim assessments, setting goals again, reteaching, reanalyzing, and reassessing. We are losing hours, days, weeks of valuable time, when students could be doing engaging work and teachers could be collaborating on improving their craft. Data analysis should be done by central administrators, rather than crowding out the time that teachers could spend on the real work.

How did we get here? How did educators in the United States reach a point where we are, incongruously, using a completely different set of practices to help adults learn to be great than any other field? We believe there is an answer.

Our contention is that schools in the United States developed over many years as institutions where teachers work largely in isolation. Teachers plan their own lessons, organize their own classrooms, and work with their own students. The nature of teaching—a task that is done by a single adult in a room with students—was assumed to be a solitary, one-person job.

But this was the mistake that led us along the wrong path. In reality, teaching is no more solitary than any other job. Legal briefs can be written by one lawyer alone; patients can be treated by one doctor alone; pipes can be repaired by a plumber working alone. Journalists, accountants, and engineers could be organized to work solo. But despite the fact that all of these jobs could be done by one person working alone, *all were deliberately designed so that the work is done in groups, teams, or apprenticeships.* They were organized so that the planning, writing, training, diagnosing, discussing—all of the real work, with the patients and clients—is done by experts and newer colleagues working together. Teams are created to improve the quality of the work, to create collegial organizations that maintain high standards for one another, to solicit input from multiple experts, and to mentor and develop new members of the profession. Work is not done alone. It could be done alone, but it isn't. Ask someone at a law firm if cases would be better assigned to one attorney (instead of a team), or ask a pilot if a plane would be flown more effectively by brand-new pilots who had never apprenticed as a copilot. The notion is absurd.

Education should be no different. In the end, a lesson is typically taught by one teacher. But the other work does not need to be solitary. Classrooms can be shared; lessons can be written in groups; curriculum can be designed as a team; discipline and data can be analyzed as a normal course of the daily work of the team; colleagues can routinely watch each other work, as a part of a team that maintains the quality collectively for all children they serve. New teachers can write first drafts of lessons, while the master teacher on the team can edit, modify, and correct the mistakes of their apprentices. The work of a school could have been designed to be done collaboratively in groups. But it wasn't.

Recently, some educators seem to have recognized the problem—the lack of opportunities for collaboration and teamwork in education—and are adding a series of Band-Aids to cover up the problem. In fact, teachers still do virtually all of their work alone. We add a Band-Aid by scheduling a weekly training session after school, although we still do not collaborate to plan tomorrow's lesson or grade today's classwork. We add a Band-Aid by scheduling a monthly observation by a supervisor, although that supervisor isn't a teammate who works with you at any time during the rest of the month. We add another Band-Aid by providing two hours of "mentoring" from a teacher in a different grade, although this mentor doesn't work collaboratively with you on any of the work you normally do. And we add yet another Band-Aid by scheduling a meeting after school to analyze schoolwide data trends, although the data analysis isn't a part of the work you really need to do that day. Indeed, the trend among educators nowadays is to talk about the importance of "teams" and "collaboration" in every possible context (e.g., PLCs, inquiry teams, data teams, grade-level teams, planning teams, and countless others). But in schools, we are often putting new groups of adults in a room, at the same time, to do new work that wouldn't otherwise be done. Calling it "collaboration" doesn't make it so.

The result is a disjointed patchwork of "fixes" to a system that should have been restructured. A small group of adults—three or four is best—should work as a team to educate a group of 7th graders in social studies. They should work on the curriculum, write the lessons, edit and improve their work as a team, organize and decorate their classrooms, discuss and strategize about how to work with challenging students in their classes, analyze data when they review student work every day, and serve as mentors for the newest member of their team while they do all of this daily work. This is how we foster greatness everywhere—by working closely in small groups that include someone whose work is already great. Artisans teach their apprentices. Apprentices work alongside artisans for years while they hone their craft.

We contend that schools need to stop adding more new work for teachers to do in newly created groups and partnerships, in an artificial attempt to create "collaboration"—and instead, reorganize the real work teachers already need to do every day, creating authentic teams. It is easy to miss the distinction. PD sessions and feedback cycles appear to involve teachers "working together," just as teams appear to function in other professions. But one is collaborative and one isn't. We believe understanding the root of this distinction begins the path to improving teaching in a substantial way.

# References

Bassi, L., & McMurrer, D. (2007, March). Maximizing your return on people. *Harvard Business Review.*

DuFour, R., & Fullan, M. (2013). *Cultures built to last: Systemic PLCs at work.* Bloomington, IN: Solution Tree.

Dweck, C. (2007). *Mindset: The new psychology of success.* New York: Ballantine Books.

Gates Foundation. (2013). Asking students about teaching. MET Project. Bill & Melinda Gates Foundation. Available: http://k12education.gatesfoundation.org/wp-content/uploads/2015/12/Asking_Students_Practitioner_Brief.pdf

Gladwell, M. (2011). *Outliers: The story of success.* New York: Back Bay Books.

Lewis, M. (2004). *Moneyball: The art of winning an unfair game.* New York: Norton.

Marzano, R. (2005). *School leadership that works: From research to results.* Alexandria, VA: ASCD.

Marzano, R., & DuFour, R. (2011). *Leaders of learning: How district, school, and classroom leaders improve student achievement.* Bloomington, IN: Solution Tree.

National Center for Education Statistics. (2016). The condition of education. Available: http://nces.ed.gov/programs/coe/indicator_cpa.asp

The New Teacher Project. (2015). *The mirage: Confronting the hard truth about our quest for teacher development.* Available: www.tntp.org/publications/view-the-mirage-confronting-the-truth-about-our-quest-for-teacher-development

New York City Department of Education, Office of Performance and Accountability. (2016). Graduation results. Available: http://schools.nyc.gov/Accountability/data/GraduationDropoutReports/default.htm

Reeves, D. (2006). *The learning leader: How to focus school improvement for better results.* Alexandria, VA: ASCD.

Schmoker, M. (1999). *Results: The key to continuous school improvement* (2nd ed.). Alexandria, VA: ASCD.

Schmoker, M. (2011). *Focus: Elevating the essentials to radically improve student learning.* Alexandria, VA: ASCD.

Senge, P. M. (2006). *The fifth discipline: The art and practice of the learning organization* (rev. and updated ed.). New York: Doubleday.

Shulman, L. (2005). *The signature pedagogies of the professions of law, medicine, engineering, and the clergy: Potential lessons for the education of teachers.* Available: http://www.taylorprograms.org/images/Shulman_Signature_Pedagogies.pdf

Spillane, J. (2011). *Diagnosis and design for school improvement: Using a distributed perspective to lead and manage change.* New York: Teachers College Press.

Zimring, F. (2013). *The city that became safe: New York's lessons for urban crime and its control.* Studies in Crime and Public Policy. New York: Oxford University Press.

# Index

The letter *f* following a page number denotes a figure.

# About the Authors

  **Kenneth Baum** and **David Krulwich** have served, respectively, as the first and second principals of the Urban Assembly School for Applied Math and Science (AMS), a nonscreened public school serving grades 6 through 12 in the South Bronx. Founded in 2004, AMS serves one of the most underserved communities in the country and over the past decade has consistently earned among the highest possible ratings in virtually all measures.

The school has been featured twice in *The New York Times*, *New York Daily News*, *Urban Educator* (Council of the Great City Schools), *NYC's Guide to the Best Public Schools* (Teachers College Press), WCBS-TV, WABC-TV, NY1-TV, Education Update, The Teaching Channel, Univision 41, and *Folha de São Paolo* (Brazil's largest-circulation newspaper).

Kenneth Baum is an educational consultant based in New York City. He is a former principal and superintendent and has worked as a stock broker, river rafting guide, and math teacher at the middle school, high school, and collegiate levels. He served as founding principal of AMS from 2004 to 2012.

David Krulwich has worked as a litigation attorney, 7th grade math teacher, math coach, and assistant principal, and he became principal of AMS in 2012. He lives in New York City.

## Related ASCD Resources

At the time of publication, the following ASCD resources were available (ASCD stock numbers appear in parentheses). For up-to-date information about ASCD resources, go to www.ascd.org. You can search the complete archives of *Educational Leadership* at http://www.ascd.org/el.

### ASCD Edge®

Exchange ideas and connect with other educators on the social networking site ASCD Edge at http://ascdedge.ascd.org/

### Print Products

*The Art and Science of Teaching: A Comprehensive Framework for Effective Instruction* by Robert J. Marzano (#107001)

*Building Teachers' Capacity for Success: A Collaborative Approach for Coaches and School Leaders* by Pete Hall & Alisa Simeral (#109002)

*Ensuring Effective Instruction: How do I improve teaching using multiple measures?* (ASCD Arias) by Vicki Phillips & Lynn Olson (#SF114043)

*Instruction That Measures Up: Successful Teaching in the Age of Accountability* by W. James Popham (#108048)

*The Reflective Educator, 2nd Edition* (#PD11OC114M)

*Teach, Reflect, Learn: Building Your Capacity for Success in the Classroom* by Pete Hall & Alisa Simeral (#115040)

*The 12 Touchstones of Good Teaching: A Checklist for Staying Focused Every Day* by Bryan Goodwin & Elizabeth Ross Hubbell (#113009)

The Whole Child Initiative helps schools and communities create learning environments that allow students to be healthy, safe, engaged, supported, and challenged. To learn more about other books and resources that relate to the whole child, visit www.wholechildeducation.org.

For more information: send e-mail to member@ascd.org; call 1-800-933-2723 or 703-578-9600, press 2; send a fax to 703-575-5400; or write to Information Services, ASCD, 1703 N. Beauregard St., Alexandria, VA 22311-1714 USA.

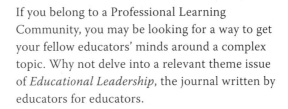

# WHOLE CHILD
# TENETS

ASCD's Whole Child approach is an effort to transition from a focus on narrowly defined academic achievement to one that promotes the long-term development and success of all children. Through this approach, ASCD supports educators, families, community members, and policymakers as they move from a vision about educating the whole child to sustainable, collaborative actions.

*The Artisan Teaching Model for Instructional Leadership: Working Together to Transform Your School*
relates to the Engaged, Supported, and Challenged tenets.

### 1 HEALTHY
Each student enters school healthy and learns about and practices a healthy lifestyle.

### 2 SAFE
Each student learns in an environment that is physically and emotionally safe for students and adults.

### 3 ENGAGED
Each student is actively engaged in learning and is connected to the school and broader community.

### 4 SUPPORTED
Each student has access to personalized learning and is supported by qualified, caring adults.

### 5 CHALLENGED
Each student is challenged academically and prepared for success in college or further study and for employment and participation in a global environment.

For more about the Whole Child approach, visit
**www.wholechildeducation.org**.

ASCD
LEARN. TEACH. LEAD.